VALLEY
OF
SHADOWS

VALLEY OF SHADOWS

By JAKE PLETT

HORIZON HOUSE PUBLISHERS
Box 600
Beaverlodge, Alberta, Canada

ISBN 0-88965-004-7

HORIZON BOOKS
are published by Horizon House Publishers
Box 600, Beaverlodge, Alberta, Canada T0H 0C0
Printed in the United States of America

CONTENTS

1
THE APPROACHING SHADOWS

The plaintive wail in the delivery room of the Royal Alexandra Hospital in Edmonton, Alberta at 5:45 P.M. on a cold day in 1942 signalled the fact that Dr. Baker had successfully delivered another child. The baby girl born to Metro and Freda Sherstanko on January 21, weighing in at 6 pounds, 13 ounces was their fifth child, the fourth girl in a row. She was destined to be different. She was cuter than all the others, with dark eyes, which later turned a hazel color; she had a dark complexion and long, heavy, dark hair. All the others were born blonde.

Her mother commented, "When they brought her to me the next morning all wrapped in a blanket with only the dark face and dark curls showing, I thought they had brought me the wrong baby." The distinct physical difference was a source of many jokes all through her life.

The family lived in Brosseau, Alberta, close to the Saddle Lake Indian Reservation, and often had Indian laborers on the farm. Her brother, Bill, used to tease her that one day as a wagon full of Indians had driven by the yard, the dogs had run out and scared the horses, which had taken off so fast she had fallen off the back of a wagon. That was how she had come to live with the Sherstans. The thought caused her many tears as a child.

She was registered in the Bureau of Vital Statistics as Mary Annie Sherstanko. She disliked all three names, so when the family changed its name to Sherstan, she began to go by the name, "MaryAnn." If ever I wanted to raise her ire I just called her, "Mary." Those were fighting words with her. Her name was never changed officially, but on her marriage certificate she was registered as, "MaryAnn Sherstan." That was the name by which I knew her.

There were other differences besides the physical ones. According to her mother, MaryAnn was mature much beyond her years. She taught a Sunday School class in the Two Hills (Alberta) Evangelical Free Church when she was still in high school, and the kids in her class were almost as old as she was. She was slow in many ways. She often told me that she was the last to finish her meals. But when it came to obedience, she outranked all the rest of her family. Her mother states, "I never had the discipline problems with her that I had with some of the others."

She was married at nineteen years of age—much younger than any of the other members of the family. When I went to see her parents at Christmastime of 1960 to ask for her hand in marriage, one of their objections was that she was too young. But at nineteen she was more mature than many women are at twenty-five and she proved it throughout her life. She was a wonderful companion, a faithful wife, and a devoted mother.

What neither MaryAnn nor any of us knew was that she was destined to be different in yet another way. Her life was to be snuffed out in a sudden, senseless

8

outburst of violence in a lonely clearing near Looma, Alberta. Her body was to be left to the elements and animals along a dirt road in heavy timber near Fort Assiniboine, by a man who did not know her, who had no apparent motive except a desire to kill, and who at this point is still at large in spite of a massive manhunt by police.

The purpose of this chapter is to describe the long chain of events and the numerous decisions which were made, which when looked at in retrospect, take on the shape of a giant funnel leading to that fateful, fatal appointment on September 15, 1971. Unknown to us, approaching shadows were looming on the horizon of our lives. Shadows that would totally envelop us for many months. But at the time we were too happy in the sunlight to notice.

I first met her at the front door of her high school on the eleventh day of May, 1960. I had just completed my third year of Bible College at Prairie Bible Institute and had come to Two Hills, Alberta to serve for one summer as student minister of the small Evangelical Free Church. When she heard I was single she determined to keep her cool distance. Yet she later admitted to me rather reluctantly that the first thought that went through her mind on the school steps when she saw me without a belt in my trousers was—and remember it was our first meeting—"Well, I could soon change that!" I never let her forget that one.

She was the president of her church youth group. As a student minister I was not getting a very large salary. Since her father was on the church board, I used to work for him on the farm to make a little extra money for tuition fees for my last year of college. On such days I would stay overnight in their home. Somehow this youth president required more

9

and more "pastoral counselling!"

When I came to Two Hills she was in her final year of high school. She had planned to leave the following fall for nurses' training. But then she decided against it (for one thing, not all her grades were high enough). Then, too, as the summer months progressed and she and I had occasion to work together in church work, her thinking began to change.

I can still remember the time her mother came into the kitchen at about one o'clock in the morning. I was sitting on the floor in the pantry door; MaryAnn was sitting on the kitchen table swinging her legs as we covered a whole wide range of subjects of mutual interest. I was growing fond of her and was pleased to see that she was growing fond of me. I have often reminded her father that he paid me an hourly wage to court his daughter!

By the time I was ready to return for my final year of college, we were both reasonably sure that we were meant for each other, "for better or worse," until death would separate us. The next year she enrolled at my college. I have often wondered how different our lives would have been if she had gone to train as a nurse.

On October 21, 1961 we pledged our love to each other in the Two Hills Evangelical Free Church and embarked on what was to be a very happy, but short-lived, marriage. We spent three years together serving in the Evangelical Free Churches of Lac La Biche and Hylo, Alberta. It was while we were in Lac La Biche that our first son, Nelson Daniel, was born on September 21, 1963. He tipped the scales at 6 pounds, 14 ounces and brought us much happiness.

In April of 1964 we moved to Taber, Alberta, where we served the Evangelical Free Church until June

30, 1967. Lyndon Andrew, our second son, weighed in at 9 pounds, 9¾ ounces in the Taber Hospital April 5, 1966 and immediately began to throw his weight around. At the time we were hoping for a girl, but looking back I have been grateful many times for two boys, because I am sure that as a widower I would have found girls much more difficult to take care of than boys.

In July, 1967, we moved to Edmonton, Alberta, hoping that I would be able to take some further training. That again proved to be a crossroads decision for us. I wanted to move to Calgary, and enroll in the University there. I knew that city better and a number of my family lived there. But MaryAnn liked Edmonton and disliked Calgary. We finally made our decision and on July 1, 1967 we arrived in Edmonton, where MaryAnn's family lived.

Since I had only a grade nine diploma it was necessary to do some catch-up work. Preliminary inquiries in Lethbridge about the Canada Manpower retraining program led me to understand that I could begin the first three-month term in July, 1967. But when I arrived in Edmonton, Manpower knew nothing about me. Since that meant a long delay, I got a job and enrolled in one correspondence course. After finishing that subject, I enrolled in two night courses the next term. It was not until six months later that I heard from Manpower again, but by then I was making it on my own.

MaryAnn was working as a saleslady for the John Rudin Company, selling a set of nine books called **Book of Life** and earning about $100 a month. When after ten months it became necessary for us to vacate our rented premises, we began to look for a new home. We were living in a small two-bedroom house which had a small basement suite rented to an elderly couple. Because we had a lot of things to store, we could open any closet in the house and expect an avalanche almost every time!

Rental properties were at a premium right at that time, so MaryAnn began talking quietly about buying a home. I was not in favor because we did not plan to stay in the city that long. She was not that easily distracted. She used to read all the "For Sale" ads, and we took many rides with agents to see properties, all of which were unsuitable.

We both believed that it was possible to enjoy a personal relationship with God. We often prayed sincerely for daily needs. One day, unknown to me, MaryAnn put her Lord to the test. Early in the week she began to pray for a home to be provided before the week was over. She reasoned that while she was at it she might as well make it worthwhile—so she specifically prayed for a house with three bedrooms. Each day she prayed and each day she read the ads in **The Edmonton Journal**.

On Saturday of that week she saw an ad describing a three-bedroom house with a bath and a half. She called the salesman immediately. He said the house was still available, but had just been listed and would not last long. She expressed her desire to see it and was told she could. A bit later that evening she called him again and said, "When can I see it?" She was sure that was it and did not want to miss it.

He said he had a sales meeting Monday morning, but would call her as soon as the meeting was over. She would be the first to see it. We decided that if she liked it, I would take time off from my job to see it too.

On Monday morning she saw the house and liked it. Feeling we could handle the financial arrangements, we became the proud owners of our first home—a two-story, half duplex. Her faith had triumphed—it even had a half-bath. On May 1, 1968 we moved in.

And the still unseen shadows moved even closer. When we bought the house we agreed that I would make the mortgage payments and MaryAnn would make the payments on the bank loan we had taken for the down payment. But as the time approached when I would be finished my high school courses and would need to prepare for university, we both realized that our financial arrangements needed some major adjustments if we hoped to avoid large debts. MaryAnn decided to do something about it.

I came home from work one day and MaryAnn was all excited. "Guess what?" she said as she came to welcome me home in her wifely fashion. "What?" I asked. She replied, "I'm going into Real Estate!" My reaction took her by complete surprise. I threw back my head and let out a big, "Ha! ha!" I thought she was joking.

I knew that she had been encouraged by a number of business people over a period of months to enter the Real Estate sales field. We had discussed it and she had always felt and I had agreed that she did not have the business knowledge to make a go of it. However, on that particular day, while she was downstairs washing clothes, she had experienced a sudden, strong urge to check the **Journal** for job opportunities in Real Estate.

Among several others, she had found one from Wilroy Real Estate, who were opening a new office in the Glengarry Shopping Centre just a few blocks from home. Her interview had been with Bill Miskew, who was to be the manager of the new branch. He had been very enthusiastic and encouraging. He had told her they would train her.

So she had decided to give it a try. My initial reaction only made her more determined than ever—so on March 1, 1969 she began to work as a Real Estate saleslady.

She went at it in typical fashion. Whenever she set her mind to something, she put her whole self into it, and by the end of her second week she had completed her first two deals. With the flush of success on her forehead, she forged ahead. By the end of that first year she had paid off our loan and her manager was predicting a marvellous career for her.

However, by midsummer, after only five months, she was told that the Wilroy office would be closing down. Because that office had been so close to our home, it had been very convenient for her to be both a mother and a saleslady. The change nearly ended her career before it had really gotten going.

Her manager suggested she apply with Graham Realty and Insurance Ltd., who had an office on Ninety-Seventh Street, just a few blocks from our house. She made an application there in July but was turned down flat. They simply did not hire female sales staff.

Everything was in limbo for about a week before Ivan Carlson, Graham's sales manager at that time, called her back for an interview. They had had a change of mind. It was becoming apparent that ladies were doing well in sales and since they would have to change their policy sooner or later, they might as well do it then. That was a giant obstruction out of the way, and in August, 1969 MaryAnn settled in once more to pursue her new career.

This time, however, it was not so easy. She managed three sales by the end of the year, as compared to eight sales and two listings with Wilroy from March to July. Undaunted, she came in with a bang in 1970, showing five sales in January alone. By May 1 that year she placed nineteenth in the top twenty "Multiple Listing" Real Estate salesmen in the city. By the end of the year she had won a trip for two to Hawaii, which we were unable to take because of my studies. Instead, she took the alternate choice of a $900 colour television and we arranged our own trip to Disneyland in May, 1971.

Her record continued to improve and by August, 1971 she was twelfth in the top twenty Real Estate salesmen in our city. By September 15 she was only a few sales away from winning a second trip to Hawaii, which of course was never to materialize. Her honesty in business and the genuine concern she showed for her clients was her best advertisement. Most of her contacts were coming as referrals from satisfied home owners.

With all that success and the financial benefits that accrued, she began to talk about redecorating our home. I was very hesitant because neither of us had time to do the work ourselves and it costs money to hire a painter. At the time, I had two student loans, she had a bank loan with which we had bought her a new car, and we had a personal loan from her father. I didn't want to be saddled with any more debts. But in her own determined way she just kept on selling so that soon I had to consent.

Our decision to redecorate the house, a decision which involved buying new drapes for the kitchen, was a major move toward her final, fatal appointment.

As she began to look for material for those drapes, two possibiiities emerged. She could get her material at either the House of Decor or Woodward's

15

Northgate. Both stores were equally close to home, the material was the same, and the prices were comparable. Her decision, however, to buy from Woodward's proved to be crucial. We waited for over six weeks for the material, with no drapes on the kitchen windows. When it finally arrived she discovered to her dismay that she was one full panel short. Instead of ordering four panels the store had ordered only three. I can still hear her saying as we discussed it, "I'm not going to let it upset me, because I know the Lord has a definite purpose in allowing it." Here she showed again her complete faith in God, Who, she believed implicitly, was directing her affairs. She was right.

When she went to talk to the manager of Woodward's drapery section, they worked out the drapery problem satisfactorily, except for a further waiting period. In the course of the conversation, she discovered that the drapery manager, Grant Nelson, was a potential client. He had an acreage near Looma, Alberta which he wanted to sell, and when it sold, he and his wife, Joyce, wanted to buy a home of their own. Renting was getting the best of them and after all it was time for them to own their home.

On July 27, 1971 MaryAnn sold the Nelsons a home. They had decided to arrange temporary financing until the acreage would sell because they had found "their" home. That of course put some pressure on MaryAnn to sell the acreage, which she listed August 19, 1971 and advertised in the normal routine. I don't mean to give the impression that pressure was coming from the owner. It was simply part of MaryAnn's desire to do her absolute best for people who trusted her to handle their very important financial transactions. If they depended on her, she wouldn't let them down.

16

She advertised the property regularly. The caption appearing most often was, "Just 19 miles from Bonnie Doon." There were a lot of calls in response to those ads, but only one seemed to be a genuinely interested client. "James Cooper," as he called himself, said he represented a large American Company. He told her he was stationed in Winnipeg, Manitoba and was looking for an acreage where he could build a large shed to store some heavy pumping equipment. He was always in a hurry. He would say, "I just flew in from Winnipeg on business and have only a few hours. Could we go and see it?"

The first time she showed him the acreage was on August 23. She later admitted to Norm, her manager, that she had been a bit concerned about being out there alone with him, and had let him walk in alone. He was always well-dressed in a business suit, very talkative, friendly, joked and laughed a lot, and made fun of the Edmonton football club. He could talk at length on almost any subject. He wanted to know the exact boundaries of the property, so after the first appointment, MaryAnn and the vendor, Grant Nelson, drove her car all over the acreage to find the surveyor's stakes and cut lines.

Her second appointment with Cooper was on September 9. She drove her car all over the acreage again, this time with Cooper, to show him the boundaries. She had met him at the Bonnie Doon Shopping Centre at 6:30 A.M. because he had said he had another appointment that day. He had called the previous afternoon and wanted to go out at 6:00 P.M. I had suggested to MaryAnn that it would be dark by the time they got there. Since he supposedly had to leave the city again early the next morning, 6:30 A.M. was the only time available.

17

He wanted to know the size of an area of land which was partly surrounded by trees. He said he wanted to see if it was large enough for his big shed. She had not had a tape measure with her, but had agreed to later come back and measure it for him. If it was big enough, he would make her an offer the next time he came into the city.

Later that day, she returned to the site with Gail Cote, another saleslady from the same office, and found that the partial clearing was too small. From a map, they then located a clearing completely surrounded by trees, a clearing which would be large enough for the client's shed.

On the day before her final appointment with Mr. Cooper, MaryAnn met Mr. Nelson again and discussed the property. He and his wife were in difficult circumstances. Joyce Nelson was not well. The interim financing was making things rough for them and he was anxious to sell. MaryAnn came home that afternoon and told me about it. Her words were simply, "I've got to sell that acreage for those people. I got them into it and I've got to help them." Again her determination came to the fore. She would have to get hold of Cooper again and get that deal put together.

The shadows were now almost upon us. That night we stood in the archway between the kitchen and the living room and watched as the pictures of the missing couple from Holden, Alberta, Mr. and Mrs. Clint Armstrong, were flashed on the television screen. They had been missing for ten days then. MaryAnn said, "How can a couple and their car disappear so completely without a trace?" We didn't know then, but the next day her time too would run out. She would be the next to disappear. The next day would be the day when all the preparations would culminate in the final drama.

Thinking back again over those days, I wonder if she might not have had some premonition of what was to come. For about a month before she disappeared, she had been taking time in the mornings after the boys were outside playing and before she went to work, to read her Bible and pray, seeking the inner strength to meet the challenges of each new day. I remember how she said to me on several occasions, "I have really enjoyed reading in First Samuel."

Thinking about that after she was gone, I picked up her Bible and turned to the book of First Samuel. There were many portions underlined in pencil. Almost all of them referred to her personal relationship with God. Such things as trust, obedience, love, service, and attitudes. One verse says: "But the Lord said to Samuel, 'Don't judge by a man's face or height, for this is not the one. I don't make decisions the way you do! Men judge by outward appearance, but I look at a man's thoughts and intentions' " (I Samuel 16:7,LB). The whole trend of her meditation during that last month seems to have been on the importance of being personally acceptable to God, Who knew her inmost thoughts.

During her last weeks she systematically paid up all her debts. In July she paid up the bank loan we had taken to purchase the car. She had owed her brother Bill ten dollars for some time. She paid that back. Her mother had done some baby-sitting for us without accepting any pay. MaryAnn said, "If she won't let me pay her, I'll just go and buy her a hat and then she has to take it as a gift." On September 13, she presented her mother with a new hat, saying, "It feels so good to have all my debts paid up." The first time her mother wore that hat was to

MaryAnn's funeral.

Perhaps, subconsciously, MaryAnn had a premonition.

Mom Sherstan related to me that she had been very concerned about MaryAnn's working evenings. When she had mentioned it to her daughter on one occasion, MaryAnn had said, "Mom, don't worry. When I go out in the evenings, I always take both the husband and wife to see the property they are interested in." Apart from one farm and two acreages she had listed, she worked strictly residential properties and so dealt mainly with couples. However, her mother said she had a feeling all that summer that something was going to happen.

I had a little private fear of my own. By September of that year, MaryAnn was within a few thousand dollars of winning another trip to Hawaii. We were looking forward to going this time if she won it. One night I dreamed she had won her trip and we were flying across the ocean with the boys. Suddenly, the plane began to go down. In my dream, MaryAnn was off to one side while I had both boys on my lap. As we realized what was happening, I clutched both boys to me and uttered the words, "Oh, Lord."

I awoke trembling with fright. I do not believe that dreams are anything more than the workings of the subconscious mind, but somehow I couldn't get that one out of my system. Secretly, I was afraid that if we took the trip, something tragic would happen. Call it premonition if you like, I really don't know. But I did utter the words, "Oh, Lord," many times during my sojourn in the shadows.

Two other things are interesting in retrospect. My family had been talking about a reunion for some time. First, we had wanted to meet in the fall of 1970 on the occasion of my parents' fiftieth wedding anniversary. When that proved to be impossible, we planned to meet at Christmas of 1970, but again not all the families could come. All that summer whenever the subject was discussed MaryAnn and I seemed to be the ones who were most anxious to have such a gathering soon. My dad was sick with suspected cancer and we somehow knew that if we were going to meet before the family circle was broken, it would have to be soon.

On Sunday, August 29, 1971, my parents, all seven daughters and their husbands, all five sons and their wives, and all thirty grandchildren gathered in the El Rancho Motor Hotel in Lethbridge, Alberta for what proved to be a very memorable occasion. In my remarks that day, I reminded everyone of how grateful we should be that although there had been serious illness at times, fifty-six of us were still living. But before the pictures taken that day were processed and mailed to each family, one face was already missing. Father was still living, but MaryAnn had broken rank on earth and become the first member of the family circle in heaven.

The other interesting thing is simply that we had an urge to travel during that summer of 1971. In April and May we made a trip to Disneyland in California. On the long weekend of August 1, 1971 we visited several family members in Gem, Alberta. Then came the family reunion. On the Labor Day weekend of September 4-6 we made our last trip together to Calgary and spent a very enjoyable three days with family and friends, unaware of the shadows which were rapidly closing in around us.

We settled down then and Nelson started his third year of school and Lyndon entered kindgergarten. I registered for my third year of university and

MaryAnn went back to work.

Contact with the client who would be responsible for hurling us into the shadows had already been established.

II

STEPPING INTO THE SHADOWS

There was nothing unusual about the way that day began, except that we both remarked that we had slept restlessly. I was just starting back to university and was trying to readjust my schedule from summer to winter routine. In summertime, I was working in construction. The heavy physical work often left me very tired and in need of extra sleep. Consequently my days began just early enough to have my usual breakfast and go to work.

During the university term, however, my practice was to study for awhile at night and retire early. Then, rising at 5:00 A.M., I would wash my face with cold water, do some exercises on the slim-gym, and then study for two hours without interruption. It did take some effort, though, to readjust to the early hours. Since the university term was only beginning and studies were not yet very heavy, I did not arise early that day. We both arose to get me to a nine o'clock class. In spite of the restless night, we faced the day as just another ordinary day.

I went to wake the boys because we liked to have breakfast as a family. MaryAnn went downstairs as usual to prepare breakfast. As was our practice, we read a Bible passage, a short explanation in a devotional booklet named **Daily Bread**, and prayed

23

together as a family. That morning we read Hosea, chapter fourteen. The accompanying article was entitled, "The Beautiful Christian." I remember reading it and wondering just how it might apply to us as a family and as individuals. The "Thought for the Day" was, "The living Christ in a yielded man is a beautiful sermon." Looking back, I think I was being prepared for the severe test ahead.

In order to make our devotional time more interesting and meaningful, we had compiled a small album of missionary pictures. Each morning one of the boys would take a turn assigning one missionary or missionary family to each person, and we would pray for them and commit ourselves and the day to God. That morning MaryAnn was particularly concerned about the Real Estate property that needed to be sold. Because "Cooper" was the only client really interested in the acreage, it was most natural that he was included in her prayer that morning as she asked God to move that property for her.

I remember so clearly how she prayed that morning. She had done it before with good results. "Lord," she said, "I need to sell that acreage. You know the problems which the owners are having. Let Mr. Cooper phone me back." She hesitated there for a moment and then added, "this week." She did not realize how soon, nor how, that prayer was going to be answered. Cooper's call came around 10:00 A.M. that day and God's call to her came about two hours later, when she passed into eternity.

Breakfast that day was the usual cereal and coffee, which we ate somewhat hurriedly so that I would not be late for my class. An interesting thing happened that morning. Again it makes one wonder whether she had a premonition of what was to come.

I had gone upstairs after breakfast to get dressed for class. Coming back downstairs, I walked into the kitchen, buttoning up the sleeves of my squall jacket. One of the buttons was coming loose. We had a thing about loose and missing buttons in our house. It was a standing joke that I would have to remind her several weeks running about missing buttons before she ever got around to sewing them back on. I would usually say something like, "Did you ever hear of such a thing as a missing button?"

That morning, though, she noticed my loose button herself and said, "Here, let me sew that on for you. If I don't do it right away, it won't get done." It was the last little deed of kindness she did for me. We laughed and joked about it at the time.

I said goodbye to her in the usual manner that morning, embracing and kissing her affectionately. That again was a normal practice for us when one of us was leaving the house for work or school or whatever. How glad I am in retrospect that it was so. Had it been done any differently it would have made the loss only that much harder to accept. As she stood by her usual place that day in front of the living-room window and waved as I drove away, we were in complete harmony with each other, with nothing between us to spoil the beautiful relationship we had enjoyed for nearly ten years.

My class in Political Science was from 9:00-10:00 A.M. Afterward I spent some time looking for text books and other supplies in the book room. I arrived home sometime after 11:00 A.M., called the baby-sitter to let her know I was back so she could send Lyndon home, and then called the Real Estate office. The secretary then informed me that MaryAnn had gone out to the acreage again with "Mr. Cooper." My immediate reaction was, "What,

25

again?'' She said, ''That's what I said, too.''

MaryAnn's manager had suggested to her that three times to one property seemed a bit unusual, especially since it involved fifty miles each time. For her, though, it was coming as an answer to prayer and she would do her part.

You see, her prayer at breakfast was being answered. She had said, ''Lord, let Mr. Cooper phone me this week.'' When she got to the office at 9:30 his call was already entered in her call book. Because she had not been in, he called again a few minutes later. She said then to her manager, ''You see, the Lord is already answering my prayer. I'm going to sell that acreage today.'' I am sure that as she went that morning to keep her appointment with ''James Cooper,'' she went in the complete confidence that God was leading her. And she was right. What none of us realized was that the Lord had also arranged for her a higher appointment which we had not anticipated.

The sudden appointment with Cooper created some scheduling problems for MaryAnn. She also had an appointment with another client at an acreage in St. Albert at 9:45 that same morning. Her manager, Norm Schultz, agreed to take one of the appointments, but he reminded her again not to waste too much time with Cooper. ''Your expenses will soon eat up your commission.''

She replied, ''I'm doing this for Mr. Nelson, and besides, I think today is the day.''

She went to her car, then returned because she had just realized another problem. It was her ''duty day,'' when she was to be in the office to take all incoming calls and relieve the secretary at lunch time. ''Norm, I'm on duty today,'' she said. ''Will you cover for me if I don't get back in time?''

From what we can piece together now, she left the office about 10:00 A.M. and came home to change her clothes. She telephoned the secretary at the company's south-side office at 10:20, cancelling an appointment she had at noon that day. As far as we can determine, she made that call from home. She then picked up Cooper at the agreed-upon place and was not seen again by anyone who knew her. It is highly probable that they went to the enclosed clearing on the acreage, where the crime was committed, and from there Cooper took the wheel.

I was home all afternoon getting settled into my routine of studies. I gave the kids lunch at noon. Nelson went back to school and Lyndon played. About the middle of the afternoon, I began to listen for the familiar sounds of MaryAnn's return. There would be the slam of a car door, the patter of steps up the walk, the opening and shutting of the house door. I would hear her familiar footsteps in the kitchen, the sound of her unloading her briefcase, purse, etc. on the table, and then she would come quietly upstairs to look for me. She would say, "Hello, you. Watcha doin'?"

But none of those sounds came. She had a habit of periodically calling her office when she was out, to check on any calls, and she often phoned home just to make sure I was getting along okay. That day she neither called nor came home. I was going to call the office several times, but persuaded myself that she was just too busy to call. I began to think about supper.

Sometime after 4:00 P.M. Gail Cote entered the office and inquired, "Is MaryAnn back yet?"

"That question just shot through me," said the manager. "I had a bad feeling about it."

Shortly before 5:00 P.M. my phone rang.

MaryAnn's manager wanted to speak to her. "She's not here, Norm," I said. "I thought she was at the office."

"No," he replied, "she hasn't come in all afternoon. I thought she might have gone straight home."

That bothered me. I said, "Let me make a few calls and then I'll get back to you."

I called the company's south-side office. They had not seen her. I called the owner of the acreage, thinking she might be at his home negotiating the sale. He had not seen or heard from her. I was puzzled. The situation was highly unusual. I called her manager back and we decided to drive out to the acreage immediately to see what we could find.

At that point I had a certain foreboding. I tried to reason it away, without much success. She could have had car trouble. But no, she would have called by now to explain the delay. Well, she could have had a serious accident. No, the police would have notified us by now. Maybe she ran out of gas. No, she was generally very careful about that. What if she was attacked at the acreage? No, that doesn't happen here. It would not happen to her.

Isn't it strange how we think that such things happen only in faraway places, say in large cities like New York, Chicago, or even Montreal, but never in a place like Edmonton? We seem to think that such things happen only to other people, people we do not know. They never happen to us or to someone close to us. Yet even while I was telling myself all that, there was a growing concern that it might indeed be happening to me.

It was my first trip out to the acreage. A very light drizzle began to fall before we got there, which merely added to the already dismal outlook. It seemed like the longest twenty-five miles I had ever travelled. As we pulled off the highway onto the secondary road leading to the acreage, I half-expected to see the familiar sight of her two-tone-green car, but it was not there. "Well, maybe she got stuck somewhere on the property," I reasoned.

The acreage was part of an old farm subdivided for sale into forty-acre plots. There were no buildings—just trees, brush, waist-high grass, and weeds. A yellow and green "Graham Realty" sign guarded the narrow trail that led back through the brush into a grassy area farther back. A small fork in the trail led right into a murky slough which was visible from the road.

Darkness was beginning to fall as we pulled to a stop. We looked for car tracks, but the ground was hard and the rain had washed away the dust, making it difficult to tell whether they had been there. We walked a short distance. What a weird and desperate feeling gripped me—I guess it was near to panic. I wanted to run and cover the whole forty acres at once. I nearly ran into the slough. I clawed frantically at the bushes, never knowing what to expect. In my mind I saw her lying helpless somewhere in that desolate wilderness.

With rain and darkness falling, I felt I had to find her. Norm went back to the car and drove onto the acreage. The brush along the trail seemed to be reaching out to engulf the car as it scraped by. We pulled into a grassy section where trails gave evidence of where MaryAnn had been showing her client all the survey pegs and boundaries the week before. Neither one of us could tell where those boundaries were. There was nothing to be found anywhere.

When we left the acreage the rain had let up. The nearest phone was about a mile down the road. We called back to the Real Estate office. I talked to Mr. Graham, the owner and president of the company. "No, there is nothing here," he said. "Did you find anything?"

"No, nothing," I answered. "Will you call the police?" He assured me that he had already been in touch with them. They were only waiting for me to call before really getting onto it. "Get them on it right away," I said. "Something has gone wrong this time."

Arrangements were made for the office staff to meet us at the acreage to intensify the search. While we waited for them, Norm and I called on some of the neighbors near the acreage. There was an occupied dwelling within a few hundred yards of either side of the entrance to the acreage. We called at both.

At the first home, we asked, "Have you people been home all afternoon?" "No," came their reply, "we just got home. We were in town all day." We said, "We're looking for a two-tone-green 1970 Pontiac with a lady driver and a male passenger. Have you seen them?" "No," they said. "Ask the lady who lives on the other side of the acreage."

Our luck was no better there. She had been working in her kitchen all afternoon. The window over her sink faces in the right direction, but she had seen nothing all afternoon. Her husband, who had been harvesting a field across the road, thought he had seen a white car with two passengers drive slowly by and then stop at the entrance. But there had seemed to be nothing suspicious about it. The next day, however, the same lady telephoned the police to say that at about 12:30 the previous afternoon she

30

had seen the car travelling slowly southward on the dirt road and the woman had looked scared. By that time the news had broken on the radio and it is possible she was afraid and changed her story so that the police would cover the area thoroughly. In any case, no other evidence ever turned up to indicate that her story was correct.

By the time we turned away from her door, darkness covered the area like a blanket. More than that, however, I had stepped into the dark shadows of the valley of deep gloom. It was a thick, smothering darkness that oozed into every fibre of my being and seemed to threaten my very existence. The rain began to fall again, not hard, but an annoying drizzle. Just enough to make you keep your wipers on while driving.

When the search party from the office arrived we went in again. This time we had a car from the Sherwood Park Fire Department with a loudspeaker, a flashing red light, and a searchlight. I struggled through the high, wet grass on foot, calling and listening. It was an eerie experience. The red light kept flashing like a beacon on a foggy night. The searchlights kept stabbing into the darkness again and again like a jungle traveller chopping his way through the dense underbrush. MaryAnn's name kept rumbling over the loudspeaker like repeated claps of thunder in an angry rainstorm.

Then, silence, in hope of a response. Surely if she were there she would see or hear and respond in some way. But what if she could not reply? Maybe the wind roaring through the trees was drowning out a feeble voice. Sick thoughts kept me slogging farther through that waste wilderness in a desperate, but futile, attempt to find her.

It was a dejected group of searchers who regrouped again at the entrance to that acreage to plot a new course of action. We were cold and wet, yet all the while I kept thinking, "What must she feel like if she is still out there?" But at night, in a strange place, under those conditions, there is a limit to what can be done. We decided on a new course of action and then set out again.

We divided into groups of two. One group went to Leduc, one went toward Camrose, Norm and I went toward New Sarepta along Highway 21 South. We checked at every service station we could find to determine if anyone could remember seeing her, or the car, or had marked down a license number, or anything that would give us a hint of where she might have gone.

You see, at that point we thought there was a strong possibility that she had been kidnapped. Norm and I stopped at three stations, two in New Sarepta and one along the highway. Each time the answer was the same—"No, we have not seen her." We thought that whether she was being driven by someone else, or was being forced to drive against her will, they would surely have had to stop somewhere. We discovered later that MaryAnn had filled the gas tank at her brother's service station just the day before and had left home that morning on a full tank.

When we had checked every station we could find, we reluctantly made our way back to the Realty office on Whyte Avenue and 105th Street. We had agreed to meet there after checking everything we could. We learned that one search party had even checked the International Airport to see if her car was parked there and checked at the ticket counter for any unusual incidents during the day. We arrived at the office at about 10:20, some five hours since I had left home. I was tired and discouraged. I had had no supper—but that didn't occur to me at the time. Each group that came in gave the same results: "Nothing! Nothing! Nothing!"

I placed a call to all the main hospitals in the city, thinking she might have been admitted. Always the same answer—"No, I'm sorry. No, Mrs. Plett was not admitted here." At that stage I would have almost jumped for joy if one of the nurses had said, "Yes, she is here. She has had a serious accident." Even that would have seemed better than what we were beginning to fear.

We called the police again and two detectives said they were on their way over. "Stay there, we want to talk to you," they said. They had no reports of any accidents that might provide us a clue to her whereabouts. I paced the office, mulling over the events. Someone suggested, "Call a radio station and ask them to broadcast the description of the missing person and the car." "No, I cannot do that. I will not release anything like that without notifying the family first. I just simply will not take the risk of them hearing the news on the radio."

We finally settled on just giving the licence number and a description of the car and asking anyone who might have seen it to call the police. It was nearly 11:00 P.M. and we were desperately trying to get through to a newsroom before newstime. I was standing near the window, leaning against the counter and staring out onto the street. Suddenly I was shot through as with lightning. There was MaryAnn's car driving slowly past the office on the inside lane!

"There's my car!" I yelled, and was out the door like a flash with the rest of them right behind me. I watched as the car proceeded west. It had only one person in it. It looked like a man, but I could not be sure. He had fairly long hair. He drove slowly at first and then accelerated quickly. He could have been trying to get a look into the office to see if there was any unusual activity there. It could also be that he merely slowed down for a red light and when the traffic light turned green, he stepped on the gas.

But by the time Wes Gregory got his car unlocked and I hopped in, "Cooper" was at least a block away. I jumped into Wes's car and when I looked up I could not see the Pontiac. Traffic was fairly heavy and by the time we got moving we had lost him. What if the traffic light had been red long enough for us to get to the car? I think I might have torn him limb from limb with my own bare hands at that stage of the incident. In any case, we had missed him and still did not know where MaryAnn was.

We headed west for about ten blocks and then turned around again. If it was MaryAnn, she would do one of two things. Either, seeing the activity in the office, she would swing around and report in, or she would turn north and head for home. We headed for my house. I felt somehow that I would find her there, but when I rang the doorbell, the baby-sitter answered and MaryAnn was nowhere to be found.

I called back to the office. She hadn't reported back there either. The hope I had after seeing the car was dashed to pieces. In place of that hope was a sickening sensation, like a block of ice in the pit of my stomach. I sent the baby-sitter home and resigned myself to wait for the detectives, who had reached the office just after I had left. They were on their way to the house. They had released an "All Points Bulletin" concerning the car four minutes after it had been sighted near the office.

Gail Cote, the saleslady from the office who had

gone with MaryAnn to measure the clearing, and Hans Rissol, another salesman, came over before the police arrived. I was grateful, because the house was very quiet and my nerves were as tight as fiddle strings. The police arrived and asked some basic-information questions, none of which I remember. Gail and I agreed to go with them first thing in the morning to search the acreage with a police dog.

After the detectives left, the three of us just sat and talked. It seemed like a horrible nightmare. I wished that I could wake up and find it wasn't true. Gail and Hans both offered to be of service in any way possible and left late that night. I was left alone. I was too distraught to even think of sleeping. Besides, if anything developed I wanted to be ready. My mind was in a whirl. Hundreds of tortured thoughts pounded their way into my mind. Like rabbits, they darted off in a thousand different directions all at once.

It seemed that in the darkness that had settled over me that night, I had stumbled and fallen into a raging torrent. Swept along in its relentless path, I had just plunged over the rim of the cataract into the boiling caldron below. I felt like a drowning man gasping for breath in the foam, clawing at anything I could get my hands onto, in a desperate attempt to lift myself from the depths of despair.

When it seemed that I just could not endure any longer, I picked up the phone and called Rev. Ed Enarson of the Missionary Church. He is not my pastor, but a very close personal friend for whom I have great respect. He must sleep soundly, because it took a long time for him to answer. But at 2:00 A.M. what can you expect? When he answered, I told him what had happened. I do not remember what he said, but I was glad to have told someone else who cared.

I had just hung up the receiver when the phone rang. The detective's voice said, "Can you get Mrs. Cote to come with us to the acreage right away? We have decided not to wait until morning."

"She just left a short while ago," I said. "I'll see if I can reach her. I would like to go too, but I'll have to arrange for a sitter first."

They obviously did not think I could get a sitter at that time of night. "You can come if you like, but we want Mrs. Cote to come along to show us the clearing which she and Mrs. Plett measured for this 'Cooper.' We think that's where they were headed."

"What time do you want to go?" I asked.

"About three o'clock," he replied. "Can you meet us here at the station by then?"

"I'll do what I can."

I was glad that they were going. Time was precious and as long as I was doing something, I did not have time to think too much. I called Gail and she agreed to come immediately. She was a jewel. She was in the middle of getting ready for bed, but she came without hesitation. I called Hans Rissol and he came to stay with the boys. When I left the house, my instructions to him were as follows: "I don't know how soon I will get back. If the kids wake up before I'm home don't tell them what happened. Just tell them I had to go out and will be back as soon as possible. If any of the family calls, whatever you do, don't tell what has happened. I want to do that myself when I get back."

You see, I had not told any of her family yet, reasoning that since there was really nothing they could do at night, they might as well get a good night's sleep. They would need it in the morning.

No one said much on the way to the acreage. The police asked a few questions, which we answered without much elaboration. That is when I first began to realize that people might think that MaryAnn had left voluntarily. Some of the questions I answered that night focused on our marriage relationship.

"How well did you and MaryAnn get along?"

"Ours had to rate as one of the best of marriages."

"Did you have any fights?"

"We had our differences at times, but we never fought or argued angrily. We always tried to talk the problem out as soon as possible."

"Did you have a fight last night or during the day?"

"No, we were on the best of terms."

I did not know it then, but I had just answered questions which I would have to answer again many times along with many others like them. The police were doing their duty and they were trying to do it thoroughly.

The police-car radio chattered almost constantly as bits of information were being channeled into a central station. One report came from an officer who the night before had been cruising by the office where MaryAnn had worked. "I saw a woman of similar description in the office and it looked like there was a party going on there about midnight."

I knew where MaryAnn had been that night! She had been with me, home in bed where we belonged. Gail then immediately clarified the point. She had been working late at night, trying to close a sale for a client.

We arrived at the acreage during the darkest part of the night—those two or three hours just before dawn. It was still raining lightly now and again, which served only to make the night more dismal.

The acreage was uninviting even in daylight under normal circumstances. But to search there in the blackness of a cold, wet, windy night under those circumstances was something else again. The grotesque and frightening spectre which loomed before my mind was the possibility of stumbling over her body in the darkness. The lights from the two police cruisers cast eerie shadows as they valiantly pierced the blackness of the night.

Our first task was to find the enclosed clearing which MaryAnn was to show her client. That proved to be more difficult than we had thought. Gail had been there only once, in daylight. But at night everything looks different, and so we spent the better part of the night trying to locate the clearing in question.

By the time we found it, it was beginning to dawn. We all got into our cars, so as not to interfere, while the policeman went to work with his dog. After receiving MaryAnn's scent from some clothing I had brought along, the dog sniffed his way around the area thoroughly. The clearing itself is completely surrounded by trees with no trail leading directly to it. On the north side is a small opening in the trees with a barbed-wire fence as a boundary. There was evidence of newly-made car tracks there, but the rain made it difficult to identify tire treads. As the dog covered that area he showed some extra interest in a spot on the northwest edge of the clearing, but raised no alarm. Perhaps the rain had washed away the contact scent.

If her death came about at the acreage, and I think it did, then it would have happened there. Probably she nosed the car up to the fence. They would have climbed through the wires into the clearing, where he then proceeded to strangle her. After depositing

38

her body in the trunk, he would have been in a hurry to get out, which could account for the spin marks as he left the area. From there he likely proceeded to a previously chosen area where he deposited her belongings and her body. There is still a measure of uncertainty about whether he used MaryAnn's car all the way to Fort Assiniboine or transferred everything to another vehicle.

After giving the police dog a rest, the officer took him through the area again, but nothing of any importance turned up. It is hard to describe how I felt as we drove away. I was disappointed because no clues had been found that would help in the search. I was glad because I could still hope that she was alive somewhere, even though she might be being held for ransom or for some other unknown reason. I was apprehensive about going home to face my boys and MaryAnn's family. I was physically tired after a whole night of searching. My mind was numb from darting in a thousand ways all at once and my heart felt like a stone.

We arrived back at the police station at about 7:00 A.M. When Gail and I arrived at my house, the boys were already up. They came running and left me no time to think anymore about what to say or how to tell them. "Dad, where's Mommy?" I was facing one of the hardest moments of my life. How do you tell two boys aged seven and five that you don't know where their mother is; that she may have been kidnapped or even murdered? Someone suggested not telling them anything, in the hope of finding her. But, I reasoned, if we don't find her and I have to tell them later, I might lose their confidence if I am not honest with them from the start.

So right from the beginning I established with my sons an open line of communication. I'm glad for that. In reply to their question, I simply said, "Boys, I don't know where she is. She went to show a man some property and we can't find the man or her or the car. The police are looking for her now and they will find her." Throughout the entire experience we always spoke honestly and frankly. I tried to answer all their many questions so that they would be able to understand. I think it proved to be the right decision in our experience.

At that point I became aware of another situation. MaryAnn's sister, Grace, was to ride with me to the university that morning. When I didn't arrive at the appointed time of 7:15 she called the house. She asked where I was.

"He had to go out."

"Is his wife there?"

"No, she isn't home either."

"Where are they?"

"Well, I can't tell you that now."

The whole thing seemed so strange to her that she called her brother Bill and by the time I got home the whole family was already on their way to the house. The fact that they arrived together was good from the standpoint that I could tell them all what had happened as far as we knew the facts and we could all be together while the initial shock registered on each one. Slowly the shadows enveloped them too. As one can readily understand, the news brought all normal activity to a standstill and for some the trip back to normal living has been long and difficult.

The police called and we talked about the possibility of releasing the news in order that the public might be involved in the effort to find some clue to the mystery. They asked for a picture and permission to release a statement. It meant calling the many relatives I have outside the

Edmonton area. I called a sister in Calgary, gave her the news, and asked her to notify all my family. We had to call MaryAnn's three sisters: Nell, in Medicine Hat; Jeanne, in Tacoma, Washington; and Florence, in Kodiak, Alaska, where I also have a sister. That took time and courage and we moved mechanically as though we were still in a dream.

Then came the first of many trips down to the police station, where details were arranged to release the news. It fell like a bombshell over the whole city, coming as it did only eleven days after the disappearance of Mr. and Mrs. Clint Armstrong of Holden, Alberta. It sent ripples through all strata of our city and led to the beginning of anonymous phone calls, which is another story all its own. It was the beginning of the most difficult period of my life, which was to last much longer than I anticipated. It would involve many things and many people still unknown to me. What had begun as an ordinary day turned out to be a day that I will never forget, a day which changed my life-style and nearly shattered me.

It was the day in which we stepped into the Valley of Shadows, where the darkness was almost overwhelming. We would walk in those chilling shadows for a long time. I would grope almost blindly at first, trying to feel my way through, but gradually I would learn to walk more confidently in the shadows because of my faith in a loving God. That faith was about to receive its most severe test.

III
A LIGHT IN THE SHADOWS

During those first few days in the darkness, it seemed I was groping around in circles. It is difficult to describe the feeling. It seemed I had lost all sense of direction. I was lost and bewildered. The chilling darkness made my body numb all over. I had no desire to eat or sleep and none of the things that normally interested me had any meaning anymore. I wanted to run outside, pick up the world, stop it in its mad rush, and shake it until it revealed the secrets that it hid in its bosom. But how does one get hold of it? One of the most difficult things in such a moment is to see life all around you going on in its normal fashion, seemingly oblivious to your soul's inner torment.

I was very fortunate to have around me family and friends who did all they could to help me in my sorrow, in spite of their own sense of loss and pain. From Thursday morning on, when I first broke the news to them, the Sherstan family was by my side constantly. No family of in-laws deserves more credit than they for the way they stood with me. We had suffered loss before, when on January 1, 1965 MaryAnn's oldest sister, Florence, lost her husband, Andrew Daneliuk, in a car crash just east of the city on Highway 16. But this was different. The blow had struck even closer home, and more difficult yet was the agonizing uncertainty which we faced together.

Bill, MaryAnn's only brother, left his work as operator of his own service station and for nearly two weeks became almost my constant companion. We were not only uncertain as to what had happened and why, but we were also afraid that if we were dealing with a lunatic of some sort, he might go after the rest of the family. I was almost never alone day or night for three weeks. There was always someone in the house besides my boys and me, night or day, and whenever I had to go anywhere during the day, Bill would drive me. I do not know how I would ever have survived those first weeks without them.

Mom Sherstan tried her best to help as well, but she was so crushed herself that it soon became obvious to us that she would need help, rather than be able to give it. They lived only about three blocks from us. She and MaryAnn used to talk to each other at least once a day on the phone, if they did not see each other in person. Because of this very close association which they had enjoyed during the three and a half years we had lived at our address, MaryAnn's disappearance came to her mother as an even greater shock.

Jeanne, MaryAnn's sister who lived in Tacoma, Washington at the time, arrived in Edmonton on Monday, September 20, 1971. She is a very practical type and I think it was she, more than any of the others, who helped keep some semblance of order and routine in the household. She was here to help us through one of the most difficult experiences of those first weeks.

Nelson's eighth birthday arrived on September 21, just six days after his mother's disappearance. We debated whether or not to give him a party, but finally came to the conclusion that we should try to make life as normal as possible for the boys. I had no heart for it, so Jeanne took over and arranged for a gathering which consisted mostly of family. Nelson got some gifts of money, which he saved to buy his hockey equipment that fall, and I presented him with a wristwatch that his mother had purchased for him the day before she disappeared.

One often wonders just what goes through the children's minds during such times. Nelson gave us an indication of his thoughts after the party. When his aunt was tucking him and his brother into bed he asked, "Do you think that if Mommy is in heaven, she saw my party and the gifts that I got?" For them it was merely the beginning of a long series of questions they would ask.

When Jeanne had to go back to her home and family in Tacoma, another sister, Nell, arrived from Medicine Hat to take over. Nell's little daughter, Lori Ann, did all that a little girl just learning to walk could do to bring some welcome and comic relief when it was most needed. By the time Nell had to go back to her home and husband, I was able to arrange for housekeeping assistance through the Family Service Association. Mrs. LeGrand came on October 4, 1971 and under difficult circumstances did a very commendable job of maintaining a household for three men.

I should also mention here that the principal and teachers at Scott Robertson School, where Nelson had just begun grade three, gave us excellent support and cooperation. It was just about that time that a boy in Ontario was kidnapped from school and was later found murdered by his captor. That only

44

added to our anxiety, and so when I took Nelson to school on the 20th of September we made arrangements with the school that he would be brought to school and picked up again at the door by someone both he and the teaching staff would know. Under no circumstances whatever were they to let him go on his own, or send him with someone they did not know. I'm sure it must have meant considerable inconvenience for them, but they cooperated very well.

Nelson had another problem which they did their best to alleviate. After a few days of school, I asked Nelson how things were going. He was rather noncommittal at first, but then he finally said, "It's just that some of the other kids keep asking me about my mom and that makes me so sad." As it turned out, it was some of the older kids who, I'm sure, were not trying to hurt him, but were unnecessarily curious. I informed his teacher of the problem and she and the rest of the staff did their best to explain to the kids that it would only be fair for them to leave him alone on that subject. From then on we had no more trouble.

It was during those first days that Mr. Graham, the owner of the company for which MaryAnn had worked, looked after a very important matter to which we had not given too much thought. In her key case MaryAnn carried keys for both cars, the house, and the Real Estate office. Since those keys were never found, we would have been very vulnerable if whoever had them had decided to use them. It was just another act of kindness that when Mr. Graham hired Joel's Locksmith to change the office locks, he also had them change the locks to the house. We received a set of new keys, and I'm sure Graham Realty paid the bill, because I never got one.

Some of the things that were most difficult at the time have in retrospect proven to be of highest therapeutic value. Before two weeks were up it became rather painfully apparent that I would have to go to work. I needed to support myself and the boys and besides, the days were getting awfully long just waiting. I did not have unlimited resources on which to draw while waiting for some new development to bring our uncertainty to an end. We had built up a small bank account over the summer and were hoping to be able to make it through the winter without another student loan. There were also some commissions still to come from MaryAnn's Real Estate transactions, the possession dates of which were still several months away. But there are expenses which one never counts on involved in such an ordeal.

I concluded that while I might be able to squeeze by financially for one year, I was in no condition mentally or emotionally to cope with the heavy studies of the third year of an honors program in Sociology. Besides, I am not the type of student to whom studies come easily. In previous winters, the boys had often complained that they never got a chance to spend time with me. Now, more than ever, I would need to be free in the evenings in order to give myself to the boys, because they were having a tough time with their own adjustments.

Consequently, on September 30, 1971, I withdrew from the university and began working for Engineered Homes on a project just seven minutes from my home, under a superintendent I knew personally. I had worked for Jack Derman before my university days when he was with another firm and I was taking night classes. He was more like a friend to me than an employer. Since I was being paid by

46

the hour we agreed that whenever I needed to go on some business regarding the case I would just let him know. That meant a lot, because sometimes new events came rather unexpectedly. He has never said so, but I am sure he must have wondered at times why I even bothered to show up for work at all!

Those first few days and weeks at work were like a nightmare. I started on a Thursday at noon. That first half-day was bad enough, but by the time I got home on Friday, my first full day, I thought I would be violently ill. All day long my mind had been concentrating on only one thing: trying to figure out some motive, trying to think of someone who might have had a grudge against us or her, imagining all sorts of gruesome possibilities, trying to convince myself that she was still alive somewhere, looking for any bit of information that might be useful in some way. Anytime I saw a mound of dirt, I could hardly resist the urge to dig it up in case she was under it. If I saw a clump of trees or a ditch I could hardly control the urge to search it. All the while I was supposed to be making accurate measurements and finding the correct levels for steel beams that were to hold up entire sections of a Senior Citizens' complex. I never counted, though perhaps Jack did, how many times I started something and before I could finish, I forgot what I was supposed to be doing.

But as I look back on it all I see that the fact that I had to go to work was very good for me. I began meeting people again. It gave me something to do rather than just to sit at home and go mad. It began to restore a form of order and routine to my life that was so essential at that time. It got me out of the house and away from the immediate surroundings that served only to remind me of all the things that

47

used to be. It was terribly hard, but as I look back now, I am glad that I did what I had to do. It proved to be far more important than I could ever have dreamed possible.

Another real source of encouragement to me was the very genuine concern shown to me and the entire family right from the very beginning by vast numbers of people, many of whom I had never met before. For some reason the case had generated an unusual coverage in the media. MaryAnn was well known and liked among her business associates and had made a host of friends.

When the response came, it came in a deluge. Everyone seemed so eager to offer help that it soon became a physical impossibility to accept it all. I tried to be as gracious as I could in turning it away, because I didn't want to offend anyone. People brought or sent food until my deep-freeze became so full that I had to pass the word around that though I appreciated everything offered, I just couldn't use it all. "Perhaps at a later date," I would say.

I still have dishes that were left at the house, but I have no idea whose they are. People called at the house, telephoned, and wrote letters and cards. It was impossible for me to reply to them all, but I cherished each one because I knew that each one was an indication of the deep concern that people had for us. Many contained the reassuring words, "We are praying for you."

We will never know this side of heaven just how many people prayed fervently and frequently for the boys and me, for the Sherstan family, for my family, for the police in their investigations, and for the killer himself, even though we were not sure at that time just what had happened. I received word from churches and individuals in many parts of

Canada, the United States, and even many countries overseas where people we had never met were praying earnestly for God to intervene.

As the story of God's grace unfolds in this chapter, I want it very clearly understood that I firmly believe that what happened in my life in terms of personal victories in the midst of tragedy is a direct result of the united and constant prayers made by the people of God for us, prayers that knew no denominational limitations.

In one letter alone, a friend referred to two church groups in northern Alberta and others in Japan who had heard the news and were deeply concerned. I have a whole box full of letters and cards indicating the genuine, prayerful concern felt by so many hundreds of people in many parts of the world.

However, as welcome as all the visits and letters and calls were, one stark fact remained. It is a simple, fundamental principle that there is a point in many of our human experiences beyond which no other person can go with us. There was no one among all the friends and relatives who could sit down beside me and say, "Listen, friend, I know exactly what you are going through, because I too have experienced an equally deep sorrow." Even if one of them could have said, "Look, I lost my wife too, some time ago," it still would have had its limitations, because each experience and each personality is different and hence the needs are different as well. I suddenly realized that there was a point in my experience beyond which no other person could go with me.

Beyond that point I would have to find the strength to go alone—with God. It was then that I finally came to the realization that God was able to begin His miracle of grace in me.

The shadows were indeed dark about me. I was groping my way through a valley I had never walked before and I could see no way out. I was desperate, alone, and afraid. But it is also true that when the shadows are deepest, light will shine the brightest. I was about to discover that there was a light that would guide me through the Valley of Shadows. God's Word declares: "Your Word is a lamp to my feet and a light to my path" (Psalm 119:105, Amplified). Had it not been for the light of God's Word, I would have stumbled and fallen in despair.

I was in such a state of numbness and shock that for the first few days I functioned more like a mechanical robot than a live person. As the events of the first four days unfolded relentlessly it seemed that the longer I groped around in the darkness, the more bewildered I became. Finally, on Sunday morning, September 19th, since I could not sleep anyway, I went into my study and closed the door behind me. My eyes simply could not penetrate the darkness. I was groping, reaching, clutching at anything that might help me to stay on my feet.

Up until that moment I had not been able to pray, but in desperation I lifted my inner being to God and asked for strength to keep me going and for wisdom to understand what was happening in my life.

That morning, though I do not necessarily recommend the technique as a good practice, I opened my Bible at random, asking God for guidance. The Amplified Old Testament opened at Psalm 32:6. The very first verse on the left-hand page engraved itself indelibly on my mind—"Surely when the great waters of trial overflow they shall not reach the spirit in him."

It was just what I needed. If I may change the figure for a moment, certainly my soul was floundering in the undertow of a seething caldron of anguish. The "waters of trial" were certainly rushing over my head as I struggled desperately to stay afloat. Yet before me in God's Word was a promise which I could claim for my own, a promise which stated that even when the waters did overflow, I would surface again and God would fill my inner being with the life-giving breath of assurance that He knew what He was doing.

He was quietly assuring me that morning that I would not be swamped. No matter how perilous the situation might be, it would definitely not be beyond my ability to endure. It was as though Jesus Himself were beside me saying, "Look, my son, I am the expert Lifeguard. You just cling with all your might to the lifeline which I hold in my nail-scarred hands and I will rescue you from the rapids. Trust Me implicitly—I won't let you drown."

I began to see things from a different vantage point. I had been thrashing about in panic, fearing I would drown, when all I needed to do was relax and float on the current of His love. As long as He was on the other end of the lifeline, He would never let me go deeper than the measure of my endurance. He and I set out that day on a new and more intimate experience than I had known to be possible.

During the next seven months or so there were many times when a specific passage of Scripture became particularly meaningful to me. With each new insight, the light shone more brightly in the darkness. Almost daily I found new strength and courage to face the needs of that particular day, to walk with greater confidence.

The passages of Scripture, as I share them, are not necessarily in the particular order in which they were experienced and they are certainly not the only Scripture passages God gave me. They are chosen primarily to demonstrate how God worked in my life, with the hope that all who face similar difficulties will be encouraged and challenged to find help in them as I did.

One of the first lessons that came to me very forcefully concerned my attitude toward this man "Cooper," whoever he is. I had never met him, or ever seen him. MaryAnn and I had discussed him only briefly after her first two appointments, so I really knew almost nothing about him. Yet whenever I thought about him, feelings of bitterness were aroused within me. I was not accustomed to such feelings and they made me somewhat afraid because I was not sure how to cope with them.

During those early days of my experience, the supervisor of the Family Service Association asked me how I was managing. She said, "Do you have someone to whom you can vent your feelings? You have a right to be bitter, you know." Well, I knew I was bitter. In fact, if I had gotten my hands on Cooper the night he drove MaryAnn's car past the office, I think I would have enjoyed skinning him! But I was not so sure I had the "right" to be bitter, as the lady had suggested, although I knew she had meant well.

Then one day, about a week after MaryAnn had disappeared, as I was reading my Bible I came to Psalm 37. The first statement in verse one stopped me in my tracks. It came like a clear and direct command from the Lord. "Fret not yourself because of evildoers, neither be envious against those who work unrighteousness...for they shall soon be cut down like the grass and wither as the green herb." Verse seven came with double force.

"Be still and rest in the Lord: wait for Him and patiently stay yourself upon Him. Fret not yourself because of him who…brings wicked devices to pass." But verse eight was the clincher. "Cease from anger and forsake wrath; fret not yourself; it tends only to evildoing."

My bitterness was not right. If I did not conquer it, it would only lead me to drastic measures—perhaps even to kill if the opportunity presented itself. Then I would be no different from the one against whom my bitterness was directed. If I harbored hatred and sought to take revenge, that would be as senseless and as loathsome to God as the original deed. I knew I had better do as God suggested and "wait for Him and patiently stay myself upon Him." He would work it out in His own way.

Again that day the Lord and I did business together. I confessed my bitterness to God and asked for His forgiveness and the strength to overcome it. He forgave and the hatred and bitterness drained out of my system like dirty water from a sink. In its place came a genuine concern for Cooper. I made God a promise that day which I have shared publicly on several occasions. I have been praying for Cooper. I promised God that when Cooper is apprehended, I will take a minister friend along with me and we will visit him. I want "Mr. Cooper" to hear from my own lips the Good News that Christ will forgive him and save his soul if he will simply by faith receive Him as his own personal Saviour. I do not bear him any malice or grudge, although I still expect that when the time comes he will have to pay the consequences of his deed.

As the hours lengthened to days and the days

stretched into weeks and the weeks became long months of uncertain waiting, I became extremely impatient for something to happen. One day soon after the disappearance, I told Detective Gowler of the Edmonton City Police Force about my concern.

We had been discussing the investigation up to that point and the prospect that as each day went by, the discovery of her body would be more unpleasant. I told him on that occasion, "You know, the thing I dread the most is that you may never find anything at all." He replied that that possibility always hovers in the back of a policeman's mind when working on a case. As we discussed the various leads I was distressed to see that one by one they all came to a dead-end. Finally the day came when Gowler had to admit to me that they had nearly exhausted every possible clue.

I shared my impatient attitude with the Lord on a number of occasions during my moments with Him in my study. But it seemed that each time I mentioned it to Him I got the same reply. I had to learn a twofold lesson of patience and trust. His promise of help and deliverance was crystal clear, but somehow was always preceded by the words "not yet."

Here are some of the passages: "Be still and rest in the Lord; wait for Him and patiently stay yourself upon Him..." (Psalm 37:7, Amplified). "Wait for and expect the Lord and keep and heed His way and He will exalt you to inherit the land; (in the end) when the wicked are cut off you shall see it" (Psalm 37:34, Amplified).

I finally cried out in near despair with the psalmist: "And now Lord, what do I wait for and expect?" And then I immediately answered my own question

54

as the psalmist had done: "My hope and expectation are in you" (Psalm 39:7, Amplified). The psalmist knew where his only hope lay. "I waited patiently and expectantly for the Lord and He inclined to me and heard my cry" (Psalm 40:1, Amplified). "Hope in God and wait expectantly for Him, for I shall yet praise Him, my help and my God" (Psalm 42:5, Amplified).

That last thought is expressed three times in the same passage. The Lord was simply saying to me: "What I am doing now you do not understand. But you don't really need to understand it. All that matters is that you have complete confidence that I know what I am doing. I won't let you down." Rather reluctantly, I must admit, I said, "Okay Lord, I can wait. But in the meantime how am I going to cope with the uncertainties, the fear, the pressures of trying to be both parents at once, the work, the weariness? Lord, the weight of the whole thing is crushing me."

And once again in His own gentle way He said: "Cast your burden on the Lord—releasing the weight of it—and He will sustain you; He will never allow the (consistently) righteous to be moved—made to slip, fall or fail" (Psalm 55:22, Amplified). There was the reason for part of my problem. In the mornings in my study as we shared those precious moments, I was telling the Lord my problems, but I was not letting them go. When I left my room I was still trying to shoulder the whole load by myself. Slowly, as I learned to leave my load on His shoulders, I became aware that His promise, "I will sustain you," was true.

It was then that I received great help from reading Catherine Marshall's book, **Beyond Ourselves**. In her chapter on the "Prayer of Relinquishment," she pointed out how one must be prepared to release all one's hopes and dreams to God and accept and embrace whatever He chooses for us. I can still remember sitting in the dressing room of the Rosslyn community rink while Lyndon was having his hockey practice. While I waited, I was reading a book. If anyone had come in that Sunday afternoon he would have wondered why a grown man would cry over a book he was reading. But in my loneliness, and crushed under the burden, I sat reading and relinquishing, as tears flowed unrestrained down my cheeks and I said, "Lord, You know best. I'll wait and hope and expect and let You carry my burdens because that is all I can do. Even though I don't understand, nothing will ever shake me from implicit trust in You; and what You ask me to endure I will endure gladly with patience"

It was during one of those quiet-but-revitalizing moments in my room that I experienced in a new way the tenderness of a loving God. Human sorrow can be so intense that it literally becomes a physical pain. For about a month or so my sorrow was like a real pain in my chest. It felt as if a football-sized rock were suspended from my heart muscles. That can be very debilitating to the system, but I found no way to alleviate my condition.

Once again the Lord stooped down and spoke in clear and unmistakable language. I read: "He heals the broken-hearted and binds up their wounds— curing their pains and their sorrows" (Psalm 147:3, Amplified). I remember it as clearly as if it were today. I said, "Lord, You are called the Great Physician. You are the great Heart Specialist. If ever a heart needed healing it is mine. If ever wounds needed binding they are mine. I am Your patient. You can establish Your practice right here and

56

now." It was as though I could feel His tender hand pouring the healing oil of His love on a wound that He had allowed, and oh, what wonderful relief it brought.

That morning, for the first time since the fifteenth of September, I got up from my knees to face a new day without that pain. The sorrow was still there, but it was different. I knew that I was in the care of the greatest Physician ever to walk the face of this earth and that my recovery was a guaranteed certainty. That day of deliverance became one of the major turning points in my life and set me on the road to recovery from a very critical condition.

October was drawing to a close and with it came the prospect of a long, cold winter of darkness without an end to the agony. Our hopes soared when two hunters discovered MaryAnn's briefcase along a dirt road in the Fort Assiniboine area. At least it gave the police an indication of where to look. But then as snows came and nothing more was found, we all settled down to wait for spring.

I had courage enough to endure the trial, but daily as I read my Bible I was impressed by the psalmists' ability to be grateful and express their gratitude to God in the midst of very trying experiences. Several new insights brought me to a new plateau in my experience. I was about to learn how to praise God in the midst of sorrow.

The first insight was simply that thankfulness is "expected" even if it does not issue voluntarily from one's being. "Offer to God the sacrifice of thanksgiving and pay your vows to the Most High, and call on Me in the day of trouble and I will deliver you and you shall honor and glorify Me..." (Psalm

50:14,15, Amplified). I had been calling for deliverance often, but I had never been able to thank Him for my circumstances. The promise of deliverance was inseparably linked to the condition that God get the credit.

It was becoming more and more obvious that if anything would happen, it would be God's doing. "But God will shoot an unexpected arrow at them and suddenly they shall be wounded. And they will be made to stumble, their own tongue being against them; all who gaze upon them will shake the head and flee away. And all men shall reverently fear and be in awe and will declare the work of God; for they will wisely consider and acknowledge that **it is His doing**" (Psalm 64:7-9, Amplified). (Emphasis is mine.)

That was the secret. God should get the credit. I renewed my promise to publicly acknowledge Him whenever I got the opportunity. I determined that I would begin to give God thanks in advance for what He was doing and what He was going to do in the future. I was, of course, thinking perhaps in terms of my own church group, but God had other things in mind.

Not long afterward, on November eleventh, I had the opportunity on CFRN radio to declare my confidence in God on the Jim Roberts open line. That was only the beginning of what God had in mind, but at least it was a beginning.

The other insight in this connection came when I suddenly discovered what God really expects of us concerning the giving of thanks amid extreme hardship. I suddenly discovered that God does not ask us to give thanks **for** a circumstance, but **in** it. "Be thankful **in** all circumstances. This is what God wants for you, in your life in Jesus Christ" (I

Thessalonians 5:18). (Unless otherwise specified, I have quoted from the **Good News for Modern Man** translation.)

Seeing that, I saw that it was possible to fulfill the requirement. I did not have to be thankful that I had lost the dearest person on earth. But having lost her, I could still be thankful for the host of maturing experiences that were coming as a result of the loss. It was about at that time that I stopped reaching out so much to others for help and began more to reach out to help those who were also in extremely difficult circumstances. I soon discovered, too, that expressing gratitude was no longer a sacrifice, but a spontaneous expression of what I really knew to be true.

Still there was one thing that puzzled me. While we were faced with some fairly convincing circumstantial evidence that MaryAnn had been murdered, none of the family was willing to concede that until it had been established beyond doubt. The problem for me was, how do I pray, if I don't know whether or not she is still living? If she were alive, then she needed prayer desperately. But if she were dead, then she didn't need prayer, having already been ushered into heaven's glory. Again the answer came simply and clearly from the Scriptures in my quiet moments in my room:

"In the same way the Spirit also comes to help us weak as we are. For we do not know how we ought to pray; the Spirit Himself pleads with God for us, in groans that words cannot express. And God who sees into the hearts of men, knows what the thought of the Spirit is, for the Spirit pleads with God on behalf of His people and in accordance with His will (Romans 8:26,27).

One thing was abundantly clear to me. I did not

59

know what to ask for. The answer was simple. Since the Spirit intereceded for me, I simply made the following arrangement: "Lord," I said, "if I pray for her safety and she is no longer alive, then simply rearrange my words and use them as a prayer for her body to be found. If I pray that her body be found and she is still alive, then Lord, she needs Your help. Then rearrange my words into a prayer that she will be encircled by the loving protection of Your presence." At that point more than anything else I wanted the circumstances to end at such a time and in such a manner that God could receive the greatest glory.

As I continued my daily readings, even though I did not yet know the outcome, I was assured of one thing—God's love. St. Paul expressed this truth so beautifully: "Who, then, can separate us from the love of Christ? Can trouble do it, or hardship, or persecution, or hunger, or poverty, or danger or death?—No, in all these things we have complete victory through Him who loved us. For I am certain that nothing can separate us from His love; neither death nor life; neither angels nor other heavenly rulers or powers; neither the present nor the future; neither the world above nor the world below—there is nothing in all creation that will ever be able to separate us from the love of God which is ours through Christ Jesus our Lord" (Romans 8:35-39).

My renewed assurance of God's love, regardless of what the present circumstances might make us think, came at a very appropriate time. It seems that whenever I gained a new insight from the Scriptures and reached a new plateau of victory in my experience, just ahead was some new test that would determine how well I had learned the lesson.

Christmas was rapidly approaching, but I think that

most of the family would rather have skipped the Christmas season that year. On the one hand, as Christmas approached, each of us sensed, in a new way, just how deep had been our loss. We all seemed to be getting more edgy and uptight, wondering what Christmas would be like without MaryAnn, because her family always got together to commemorate the special occasion. On the other hand, there was the hope, which none of us really dared to voice, that if she were still alive, possibly something in the Christmas season would cause her captor to release her. There was no doubt in our minds that if she were alive, she was being detained against her will. We knew she would never go voluntarily.

The boys and I, of course, would sense the loss most keenly. In previous years we had usually had our tree up at least two weeks in advance. There had always been presents to heighten the excitement and a leisurely time of sharing gifts on Christmas morning. We had always bought our tree together as a family. We had decorated it together. That year we went alone, bought a small tree, a new, smaller stand, and put on the decorations reluctantly. We talked about the fact that even though Mommy wasn't with us, we could still share in the true meaning of Christmas. From that standpoint it may have been one of the most meaningful Christmases we ever experienced.

About a week before Christmas the pressure was becoming almost unbearable. Once again in my room I shared my situation with my Companion and Lord. I said, "Lord, You see how things are in our home and in the homes of MaryAnn's family. Some of us are very near the breaking point. Someone is going to have to be strong and it might as well be me. Even though I still don't understand, Lord, I want to reaffirm my confidence in Your lovingkindness, Your ability and willingness to intervene in a very difficult situation."

Then I picked up my New Testament and read His answer—"And God's peace, which is far beyond human understanding will keep your hearts and minds safe in Christ Jesus" (Philippians 4:7). The answer was unmistakably clear and the experience exhilaratingly beautiful. Somehow the pressure was gone. In its place came a calm and a restfulness within my being that I could neither describe nor understand. I went to work that morning and each remaining workday before Christmas filled with singing. It just seemed to ooze out from all over. I sang out loud, I hummed tunes, I was sure someone would think I had cracked!

A few days later I was tempted to tell the Lord that He had overdone it, because I was afraid that people might get the impression that I didn't care about MaryAnn anymore. I did care, deeply, but a deep inner peace had come in direct response to my plea and I decided to make the best of it.

I was reminded of a story I either heard or read somewhere. I am uncertain of the source. Two artists were individually asked to paint a picture of "peace." One artist painted a beautiful pastoral scene. The lush, green meadow was bounded by beautiful trees. Children played under the large tree which grew on the bank of a bubbling brook flowing through the meadow. Cattle were quietly grazing in the green grass or lying contentedly in the shade among the flowers. Not a breath of air stirred a single leaf.

The other artist painted a picture of a vast ocean. A mighty tempest whipped the waves into rolling breakers that crashed relentlessly against the jagged cliffs on the shore. On the face of one of those rugged peaks was a small crevice. A small dove sat in that crevice—in perfect peace—in the midst of the storm.

Such was my experience of the "peace of God which is beyond human understanding." I was like that tiny dove. I was sitting in the cleft of the Rock of Ages, in perfect peace. Nothing could shake my repose. That solid Rock didn't shudder even once under the onslaught of the mightiest billows, and as long as that Rock stood firm I had nothing to fear.

Christmas came and went and nothing changed, except that our hope that MaryAnn would be found alive took an awful beating. I had somehow hoped that Christmas would bring a break in the case, but when it didn't, it seemed to me that any hope of finding MaryAnn was in vain.

I don't really know if my dashed hopes were the cause, but after Christmas I faced a new and very real difficulty. Right after Christmas I was suddenly overwhelmed by a deep sense of loneliness. True, people were still concerned. True, people were still praying for us. True, people still kept in touch to see how things were going—but by then the phone rang less often and people came over less frequently.

That, of course, was entirely normal. Everyone has his own problems to face, household to run, and job to perform. I knew that. But still I was lonely. MaryAnn and I had enjoyed a very good relationship and I missed her greatly.

She had not only been an excellent wife and mother; she had also been a wonderful companion. She had lived for her family and we had done many things together.

Often she had said rather wistfully, "My babies are

growing up on me so fast.'' Especially during the last year she had said repeatedly, "I just enjoy those boys so much," and she had spent a lot of time with them. She had almost never bought anything, except small incidentals, without asking my opinion. Even before buying her own clothes she would want my opinion. I used to say, "If you like it, buy it," but she would insist I come with her.

On the last evening we spent together, September 14, 1971, we went to "Northgate Shopping Centre," where we bought the kids some clothes for school. She had picked out some material for a new outfit and for the past week had urged me to come with her to see it. I had wanted it to be her choice, but she had insisted. I looked at it and expressed my preference of color and pattern. She preferred the other one. I said, "Go ahead, you're going to wear it, not me." I left her with the saleslady to make her own purchase and when she came back she smilingly showed me the material I preferred. That's how she was.

Missing such companionship left me indescribably lonely. The first time it really hit me was on the evening of New Year's Day. The boys wanted to go skating, so we went to Mayfair Park. It was a beautiful night—clear, calm, and not too cold. The ice was crowded with people. I hoped I might see someone I knew, but the only ones I recognized were my own two boys. I discovered that night what it means to be lonely in a world full of people.

I was reminded of a poem we had studied in school. The "ancient mariner," after days of floating helplessly on a calm sea, had blurted out, "Water, water, everywhere, but not a drop to drink." I was skating in and out among people, hundreds of them, I had jostled against them in the building where we had put on our skates, but not one of those people could answer my need and fill the aching void within. For nearly three weeks I staggered under the impact of the new emotion I felt.

Once again I was to learn to trust God in a more complete way. Mom Sherstan suggested to me one day that we get all of the family, including aunts and uncles, together for an evening of prayer. I agreed and said, "Why don't you arrange it?" So on the evening of January 17, 1972, we met together at the home of the Sherstans for one common purpose. We were each in need of new strength and courage to carry on the simple routine tasks of life.

Each individual had brought his own needs to that gathering and together we were going to present them to God. We prayed for the man who was the human cause of all our grief. We prayed that each one would find the courage and strength to endure. We prayed that if MaryAnn were still alive, she would be sustained and protected by the invincible hand of God. We prayed that the ordeal might end as soon as possible. And while we were praying, I found the answer to my deep-seated loneliness.

It happened rather unexpectedly, but there it was, unmistakably clear. After I had prayed and others were praying one by one, I was suddenly reminded of a verse that God had spoken to Israel long ago: "When you pass through the waters I will be with you; and through the rivers, they shall not overwhelm you..." (Isaiah 43:2, Amplified). The God Who had made that promise to His people is still the same today and He seemed to be saying those words directly to me that night. It seemed that my feet could no longer touch bottom and the lonely "waters of trial" were about to surge over my head again. But He was promising His own personal attendance. He would keep my head afloat even though my feet could not touch the bottom.

The question immediately flashed through my mind, "How do I know this is true?" It was right at that point that someone in his prayer made reference to another Scripture passage, one which portrays a shepherd scene: "The man who goes in by the door is the shepherd of the sheep. The gatekeeper opens the gate for him; the sheep hear his voice as he calls his own sheep by name and leads them out. When he has brought them out he goes ahead of them and the sheep follow him because they know his voice" (John 10:2-4).

For the first time in my life I saw those passages side by side and the insight was startling in its impact. The rest of John 10 makes it clear that the Shepherd is Jesus Christ and the sheep are His followers. As I knelt there with the rest of the family I saw in my mind's eye an oriental shepherd who is gentle and kind.

Such a shepherd never drives his sheep; he leads them. He will, I am told, often call each one by name and it will respond to his voice. On some days he will want to take his sheep to new pastures where the grass is more plentiful, but in order to do so he may have to lead them across a swiftly flowing river. If so, he will stop his sheep at the river's bank and look the situation over. Perhaps the water is deep and swift and some of the weaker animals will not be able to make it. If so, he will go up stream and with his staff in hand enter the water and probe its depths. Perhaps the water is a little shallower there, but flows just as quickly. Then he will probe with his staff and make certain that there are no deep pools into which his sheep might fall and drown. He will wade across and make certain that even the smallest and weakest can make it through. Then he will return to his sheep, and calling them to follow, lead them through the water. He will go with them, helping the struggling ones until they are safe on the other side. Not one will be lost. How will he know if they can cross safely? He will personally test the stream by walking ahead. He will know just how deep it is, and he will be assured that it will not be too deep for any of his sheep.

As I knelt there that night it seemed that the omnipotent God, Who is also the tènder Shepherd, stooped down and whispered in my ear, "My dear little lamb, I know the depths of the waters I am asking you to cross. I know that the loneliness you experience seems to be overwhelming. But look, my son, I have gone before you and have plumbed the depths and know that there is no pool in this water that will cause you to flounder. I am walking with you, so you just cling to my hand a bit tighter and we will cross safely over."

I got up from my knees that night with a different outlook. The loneliness did not go away entirely, but I knew that I would be able to live with it. It was just another event in a series that was used to test my courage and my willingness to trust God implicitly.

I do not wish to create the impression that my life was just one crisis after another. Rather, I want to demonstrate that for each new problem that arose, and they were almost innumerable, there was a new supply of grace from which to draw new courage as I exercised my simple faith in God.

One of my deepest concerns right from the beginning was for the two young boys who were now my sole responsibility. Nelson turned eight one week after he lost his mother and Lyndon was five. They were normal boys in every way and were very fond of their mother. She had spent a lot of time with them.

My problem was how to help them through that traumatic experience in such a way that they wouldn't sustain permanent scars to their personalities. I knew it was not going to be easy, to say the least. In a situation like that, one is sometimes faced with simply having to make the best of it.

The difference in their personalities showed up right from the beginning. Nelson is a very outgoing person, talks a lot, meets new people easily, and expresses his emotions without hesitation. He likes to be cuddled and shows his affections very readily, often on a sudden impulse. Lyndon, on the other hand, is more quiet, dislikes meeting new people, and hides his emotions. He likes to be played with, but not cuddled, and we often had to beg him for even a "good night" kiss. None of that had changed. But if I wanted to help them meet their difficulties, I knew I would have to take their personalities into account.

Nelson cried easily and whenever the problem got too big for him to cope with, he would climb on my lap, throw his arms around my neck, and cry out his frustrations on my shoulder. Having spent his emotions and released the tension, he could then go out and face his world again. I never tried to stop him, thinking it was a natural form of release that was good for him.

Lyndon didn't cry. In the whole seven months from his mother's death till her funeral in April, 1972, I think I can count on the fingers of one hand the times he actually gave way to tears over the loss of his mother, and one of those times was at the funeral itself. He was more like I was. He bottled up his emotions much more than I cared to see.

His first good cry came on the first Saturday after his mother had disappeared. He and his brother had gone to their Uncle Bill's house to play with their cousins. We thought it would be good to get them out of the house for awhile. Things seemed to go all right until suppertime, when the pressure became too great for Lyndon and the dam finally burst. When he started to cry, there was no consoling him. They bundled him into the car and rushed him home. I heard him as he came up the walk, letting the whole world know how he felt about the situation. But when he was finished he just began again to bottle up his emotions.

I am not one to cry much either, so I found my release in talking with people. I tried to get Lyndon to talk too, but that didn't work for him. I had decided right from the beginning not to try to hide anything from the boys. If they wanted to know what was going on, I would tell them. So each time some new news came up I read it to them or explained it to them as best I could. At first I didn't think that Lyndon was old enough to understand it all. He understood all right. But because he bottled up his feelings the pressure began to show in other ways.

He would suddenly become sullen and stubborn over the slightest thing. For example, he would sit down to a meal and everything seemed normal. Then suddenly he would just refuse to eat or talk.

I remember the first time my housekeeper came. She usually came in the morning as I was leaving for work, stayed for the day, prepared supper, and then left when I got home. When she walked in that first morning and I introduced her to the boys, Lyndon turned his face away from her. He tried to ignore her completely. He was expressing how he felt about the absence of his mother, and the presence of another woman in the house. Even after three months Mrs. LeGrand told me one day, "I just can't get close to the boys," and I know she tried very hard in every way she could. I encouraged her to keep on trying although it was difficult. Every time she walked in the door she served as a reminder to the boys that they were without a mother. I was really not sure at all that I would be able to help the boys adjust successfully.

One day as I was reading in my room I came to a passage of Scripture that proved to be a tremendous source of strength for each day. St. Paul found himself in very difficult circumstances. When he sought relief, he was given a very simple, but straightforward, answer: "My grace is all you need, for My power is strongest when you are weak...(II Corinthians 12:9). That was so similar to my need. I had prayed for a long time to be delivered from the agonizing uncertainty of the situation. I had received promises of deliverance, but always with the injunction to wait patiently and expectantly. Now, just at the point where I felt like throwing in the towel and saying, "I can't take it anymore," I was being gently reminded of that inexhaustible supply of divine grace available to me that would provide all the strength, courage, stability, and victory I needed.

The one thing I had to learn was to keep drawing on that source constantly. Just as one drink of cool water yesterday is not enough to quench my thirst today, so the grace I drew to sustain me one day was not sufficient for the next day. I would have to stay right there and draw from that vast supply as I needed it. And this I did.

When Lyndon one morning at breakfast scalded his right side and leg with boiling water it called for quick action, not panic. Just a quick prayer—"Lord, You said Your grace was sufficient. It has to include this situation." And it did. But the greatest test of the sufficiency of that grace came a little later and again involved the boys.

I mentioned earlier that I thought at first that Lyndon didn't really understand what was happening. However, it soon became obvious that he was just bottling up his emotions. Nelson often cried for his mother when I put the boys to bed. That seemed to be an especially hard time for him. Lyndon, however, never cried and I knew it was only a matter of time before the pent-up emotions would erupt in some other way.

Then one evening just after New Year's Day, it happened. I had put the boys to bed as usual at eight o'clock because they had to get up at seven to have breakfast with me. I turned in just before eleven o'clock.

Suddenly from the boys' room came a piercing scream. I was up like I was shot from a catapult. For an instant my hair must have stood up straight like the hackles of a dog.

Charging into the room I turned on the light and found Lyndon standing on his bed, his eyes wide open, stamping his feet and screaming at the top of his voice, "Mommy! Mommy! Mommy!"

One minute he would reach out to hold her and the next minute, in sheer terror, he would try to push her away. I picked him up and calmed him a bit and then realized that he was still asleep. He would alternately cling to me with all his might, shaking uncontrollably, and then, screaming again would push me away, or call for me to protect his mommy.

I took him into the washroom and turned on the light. I talked to him, wiped his face with a damp washcloth, and slapped his cheeks lightly to try to get him awake. But it was a full ten minutes before he awoke and then with a heavy sigh he just fell back into bed and went to sleep. In the morning he knew nothing about it.

71

You can be sure, though, that I didn't get to sleep that night for a long time. Next to losing MaryAnn, that experience had to rate as the most shattering of the whole seven months. But it was only the beginning. For at least a month he screamed regularly almost every night. I could almost set my watch by it. He was punctual at 11:00 P.M.

Then came the night when Nelson also started in, and before I knew it I had both boys in my arms yelling and screaming, alternately pushing me away and clinging to me like leeches. It was horrifying.

I can't remember how many times, but again and again I reminded the Lord that if He said His grace was all I needed, then it had to apply to those screaming episodes too—and it did. But each time it happened I had to be right by the source to draw just as much as I needed. The grace I had drawn for yesterday was not enough for today.

There was one wish I had then which was never fulfilled. I wished that I could have had their mother's killer come into the home just so I could show him how deep were the wounds that his senseless act had inflicted on two innocent boys. I wished I could have asked him how to begin to stabilize those two young lives again. How would he comfort two boys in the middle of the night?

I wonder if, while he was laying his clever plans for murder, he ever thought of the terrible injustice of murder, not only to the innocent victim, but to the innocent young living victims who have to bear the scars of his cruelty all their lives. I wonder if he ever thinks about it now. Even though those harrowing night episiodes have ceased, I don't think they will ever be forgotten.

We stepped into the dark, impenetrable shadows on September 15, 1971. Had it not been for the fact that God drew near in the darkness with the light of

His Word to illuminate the pathway for us one step at a time, our story would have been different indeed. How glad I am to be able to say that in His light, we learned to walk with perfect confidence.

IV

THE MEANING OF THE SHADOWS

Even though I learned to walk with more confidence through the darkness, guided by the light illuminating my pathway, one question haunted me during those first bewildering days. Why did it happen to MaryAnn? She was so young and full of life. She loved her family dearly. She enjoyed her work thoroughly. She liked people almost instinctively. She trusted people. She had no enemies. True, there had been a few unpleasant experiences with fellow Real Estate agents, but that was not unusual with keen competition. She had never come out of such experiences with any enemies. Certainly within her own office and company, while competition was keen and she had a very competitive spirit, there were never any rivalries that resulted in any serious problems.

Why should this happen to our family? We enjoyed a beautiful family relationship. If it is possible, we loved each other even more after ten years of married life than the day our marriage began on October 21, 1961. She was as fond of her children as any mother could be and they were fond of her. She enjoyed a very close relationship with her own parents and immediate family. So why should this happen to us? We were a young family. Weren't there plenty of other people who already had most of their lives behind them who could have been chosen

74

instead? There were plenty of couples who didn't get along too well. Why couldn't it have happened to them instead, and saved them a divorce? There were plenty of childless couples. Why then had my boys had to be left motherless?

There were those who questioned out of the depths of bitterness. There were others who questioned out of total confusion. I think I myself questioned out of sheer frustration. All the hopes and dreams we had had, the plans we had made, and the goals we were working toward, lay shattered at my feet like an eagle's egg dropped from a height of a thousand feet. From all around me and within me the burning question was, why? Why? WHY? It seemed like my mind was a huge cave and each time the question "Why?" thundered out from me, it echoed and re-echoed through the darkness until there were a million voices and echoes in one cacophonous chorus thundering through the reaches of my soul, rising in volume until I thought I would be driven out of my mind.

It was not until I learned to change the "why" to a "what" that some semblance of peace was restored to my confused mind.

Thinking back over those first days of torment, I think it was a letter I received that began to help me understand in some measure what had been incomprehensible confusion before. The letter was postmarked Medicine Hat, Alberta, September 30, 1971. Phyllis Reynar was a very close friend of MaryAnn's. We had known her and her husband, Alan, and their three children for a good number of years and so it came as no suprise to me when she said, "I think MaryAnn was more like a sister to me."

In that letter she told of her own confusion as she had asked the same searing question, "Why, Lord?"

75

But then she drew my attention to a passage of Scripture that, perhaps more than any other, helped me to see the whole confusing experience in a new perspective. It helped me, as it had helped her, to see that there is another side to our human experiences, a side which we do not often take into consideration.

"Do not be afraid," she quoted, "of those who kill the body but cannot kill the soul; rather be afraid of God, who can destroy both body and soul in hell. You can buy two sparrows for a penny; yet not a single one of them falls to the ground without your Father's consent. As for you, even the hairs of your head have all been counted. So do not be afraid: you are worth much more than sparrows" (Matthew 10:28-31).

Her letter continued, "It finally dawned on me that if a sparrow does not fall to the ground without **God's consent**," and she had underlined those two words, "neither would this happen to MaryAnn without **His consent**," and again she emphasized those words. "Man, that settled it all for me," she continued.

The realization that perhaps I was looking at the whole experience from the wrong perspective was soul-jarring. I realized that perhaps instead of accusing God by asking, "Why?" I should instead begin to ask Him, "What?" If God had indeed given His consent, then certainly He had had a very good reason to do so. He would never have consented to anything so shattering unless He had had some very good purposes in mind—purposes that I could not yet see, but which were nonetheless good.

As I sat with that letter in my hand, my mind went back to my early years on the farm. Sparrows were a common pest. I remembered robbing their nests many times at night when they were easily caught inside. As I grew older and learned how to shoot a rifle they made good targets for my .22 calibre Cooey

76

single shot. Over a period of about ten years, there were many sparrows that had escaped my deadly missiles, but there were always those unfortunate enough to be in the direct line of fire. They would fall to the ground—lifeless. Why did some fall and some fly away? It was because God had given His consent for some to fall and not for others. That's why I had missed so often. But the decision to let one fall and another live was made by the One Who watches and feeds the sparrows and the reasons were His own.

It is true, as the passage declares, that human life is of much greater value than the lives of many sparrows, and that is precisely the point. If God took such great concern over tiny feathered pests, then how much more concerned He must have been for MaryAnn. Yet, if God had seen fit to let MaryAnn "fall" as some sparrows had, then He had done so for a very special purpose.

And so I began to ask God, "What was your purpose?" rather than, "Why did you let it happen?" My submission to a higher will than mine brought an end to the frustration and caused me to begin a search for the purpose of God. It brought a new anticipation of what God was planning to accomplish. Her disappearnace was not an accident. It was an incident in our lives carefully designed by God's loving hand, through which God wanted to fulfill some special purpose. He had carefully measured the intensity of pain and pressure we could bear and He would never let it increase beyond the breaking point.

Over a period of seven long and trying months I discovered some of the purposes God had in mind when He designed my experience. None of the lessons He taught me was easy to learn, but all were important. As I share them here it is with the sincere prayer that they will be of help to others who find themselves overwhelmed by circumstances too confusing to understand.

In the long evenings after the boys had been tucked in for the night and I was alone, I discovered in a new way that books can be wonderful companions. I have in my study a fair number of good books and one of the most recent additions was one that members of my family had given me for Christmas. Just a thin paperback, the book, **Knowing God's Secrets**, was no lightweight in content. It seemed that the author, John E. Hunter, had known my particular, trying circumstances as he had penned the pages of his book. In the chapter entitled, "The Secret of Meeting Sorrow," I found what I needed.

He related an incident in which he was shown a painting of a lovely, sunlit, country scene. He says:

> There was color and shape and composition—all beautifully balanced—but somehow the result didn't seem real. There was a sense that something was missing in the picture. Then we were shown exactly the same picture—as it should really have been. The missing ingredients were there and the painting was completely satisfactory. As we compared the two pictures we saw what had been missing—the shadows. The first picture was a blaze of joyous light but there wasn't a shadow anywhere. As a result the scene was unreal; it lacked depth. The second painting had deep, long shadows, penetrating far into the whole scene—and it was real. It takes shadows to give balance, reality, depth and contrast to a painting. [1]

It was something I had never really considered

78

before—that the dark, impenetrable shadows engulfing our lives in those painful months were designed to give balance and meaning and reality and depth such as we had never experienced before. Very slowly, yet very steadily, the shadows of confusion were beginning to lift, as I began to discover a new dimension to life. As Hunter so ably states it:

> Here indeed is one of the greatest challenges to our faith—that God sometimes needs our suffering to achieve His purpose. If, by His grace, I can see my pain as part of God's plan—even if I cannot understand it—then somehow the shadows give depth and reality to life, and I take my place in the panorama of God. [2]

I finally stopped asking God, "Why did you allow this to happen to me?" and began rather to ask in a totally new attitude, "What plan do you have, Lord, what glorious purpose do you have in your heart that requires such pain on my part?" When I came to that point in my experience, God was able to move in and give me some insights into His wonderful plan.

One insight into what God's purposes were came while reading in the New Testament. St. Peter was writing to people who were uprooted from their homes and scattered, persecuted because of their faith in God. He reminded them of the living hope they had of better things to come, not in this life, but in the next. Then he said: "Be glad about this, even because of the many kinds of trials you suffer. Their purpose is to prove that your faith is genuine. Even gold, which can be destroyed, is tested by fire; and so your faith, which is much more precious than gold, must also be tested, that it may endure" (I Peter 1:6,7).

It is easy to say that one trusts God when all is going well, but in the heat of trial, only truly genuine faith will endure. My circumstances, then, had been so designed that in God's great crucible of trials He would be able to determine if my faith in Him were made of the real stuff.

He simply wanted me to rely on Him more fully and completely. Even as a bedridden child becomes more attached to its mother, who nurses it so tenderly, God wanted my experience to draw me closer to Himself. In fact, my experience literally drove me to God. He clutched me in His arms and pressed me to His bosom so tenderly that I knew He had nothing but good in His plan. I discovered in a new way the meaning of the words: "The eternal God is your refuge and underneath are the everlasting arms" (Deuteronomy 33:27, LB).

Once again Hunter says it so beautifully:

> The pressures from above may force me
> down, but underneath are the everlast-
> ing arms. The lower I go the nearer I go
> to the arms of the God of all comfort. If I
> reach rock bottom then I am in the arms
> of my Wonderful Heavenly Father. [3]

I learned in those inexplicable months the beauty and joy of communication with my Heavenly Father in a way I had never known before. The experiences related in the previous chapter came as a result of my being pressed right down into the everlasting, loving arms of God without any way to withdraw.

I had begun to ask what purpose God had for my pain and He had begun to slowly unfold it to me as I was able to take it in. I do not believe that the things I mention here comprise the whole purpose of God, but only those parts which He chose to reveal for my benefit. In my daily reading in the New Testament during my quiet moments with the Master, I came to another deeply meaningful passage which opened a whole new realm in my experience: "What a wonderful God we have—He is the Father of our Lord Jesus Christ, the source of every mercy and the one who so wonderfully comforts and strengthens us in our hardships and trials. And why does He do this? So that when others are troubled, needing our sympathy and encouragement we can pass on to them this same help and comfort God has given us" (II Corinthians 1:3,4, LB).

The word "comfort" has changed its meaning. Most of us use it simply to convey our sympathy. We pat a person on the shoulder and say, "Look, friend, I'm sorry this had to happen. I hope it will be over soon and will turn out well for you." But that is not a very satisfying encounter in a time of difficulty, nor is it what the above passage is really intending to convey. Hunter says the word, "comfort,"

> ...comes from the Latin **fortis** which means strength and power...The God of comfort draws near to us in a new and special way and we experience a new quality of strength and power as we are being beaten down by suffering caused by pressures from without. [4]

It carries the thought of our being infused with strength. Instead of merely coming alongside of us, patting us on the shoulder, and saying, "I am sorry, friend," God comes along and by the comfort of His own presence puts steel into our spine and starch into our muscles. At the same time He puts His own shoulder under the burden so that we will be able to endure the pressure of the trials that force us so unmercifully downward.

But all the while this is designed to be a learning process for us. As we learn with the help of God to stand firm under the pressures we face, we realize that this new and wonderful discovery is too good to keep to ourselves. This is exactly what God has in mind when He designs our trials. So that the next time we meet other people who are troubled and need our encouragement we won't pass by indifferently. Neither will we stand helplessly by not knowing what to do. But drawing from our own experience of God's strength for us, we will be able to "pass on to them this same help and comfort God has given us."

It was a new challenge to me. I had been reaching out to people and saying, "Help me." Now, God said, "Look around you. There are many people who are just as troubled as you are and more, people who don't know what to do or how to cope with their problems. You go and reach out to them and say, 'I will help you.' Share your experience with them and give them some assistance. This is why you have to suffer the torture of losing a loved one without knowing when the uncertainty will be over—because there are many other people whom you will be able to help by sharing with them your experiences."

I determined by God's grace to accept the responsibility that accompanied the new depth and meaning brought to my life by the dark shadows of suffering. I determined that in the measure that He infused strength into me, I would endeavor to do the same for others who were in need of the same infusion. What I couldn't possibly know at that time was just how soon I would be called upon to prove my new dedication, nor just how many people there were, whom I had never met before, who would need such an infusion of strength. Sometimes it is good that we don't know these things in advance. Had I known then, I would have hesitated before I even began, but since I didn't know, I was determined to do my best. I would discover it soon enough.

When I arrived home from work one day early in November, 1971, there was a telephone message for me to call Jim Roberts of CFRN radio. I couldn't imagine what he might want and I neglected to return his call. He persisted. The next day he called me at work. He was hoping to do an interview with someone from the Armstrong family (the family of the couple from Holden, Alberta who mysteriously disappeared shortly before MaryAnn's disappearance) and with me to give his listeners an in-depth look at how the people closest to these two much-publicized tragedies were coping with their difficult situations. Would I be willing to come to the station the following night for such an interview?

I agreed somewhat reluctantly. I had very mixed feelings about it. Such a situation can be very painful and I was hesitant for that reason. On the other hand, there were so many people who had expressed to me their deep concern and shared that concern in so many ways that I felt somewhat obligated to share some of the more personal aspects of my experience with them. The interview was one way I could accomplish that.

The program was aired on Remembrance Day, November 11, 1971. It began with a news update, with Bruce Hogle simply reviewing the events of the past two months and generally bringing the listeners up-to-date. That was followed by an interview with a well known follower of the occult, who gave his statements and predictions. Following him was an interview with a member of the Armstrong family, and then came my interview. I was rather nervous at first, but Jim is a very capable person, considerate of the feelings of others, and I soon felt very much at ease.

Among other things, I shared some of the practical problems that we faced with the children and the household in general. I was then able to share with the listeners the fact that my faith in God was firm, that I believed He had the whole situation in control, and that I was confident that when His time came He would reveal to us what now was a mystery. I commented to friends afterwards that in a sense I had gone out on a limb with God and that night I had prayed, "Lord, now Your honor is at stake. If this limb gets sawed off, we go down together." He will never give His glory to another. It was the day after the interview was aired that I had my first opportunity to infuse someone else with the same strength I had received.

After supper, as I recall, my telephone rang. By that time I was getting used to the ringing of the phone and would talk with anyone who was cordial enough to identify himself. The lady's voice sounded quite apologetic for having called. "I've thought about you all day long," she said, "ever since I heard what you said on the radio. I just can't see how you can take it as you do." I assured her that I was drawing on strength that came from God, not from myself. Then came her own story.

Several years before, their young daughter had been assaulted and strangled, an event which had come to them as a staggering blow. Just short of three years after that, their son had been killed in a tragic knifing incident involving a scuffle with a friend. If the first case had staggered them, the second had crushed them. We made arrangements that night for me to go and visit with her and her husband. It was on my second trip to their home that I began to see how God was working to put me alongside of people who needed help, so I could help them with the same help I had received.

I was sharing with them how I had come to see that my experience had come only after God had given His consent and for very special reasons. She began to laugh. I thought, "What a strange reaction!"

She said, "You are probably wondering why I am laughing."

"Yes, I am," I answered.

Then she explained. "When we lost our daughter," she said, "a minister came to see us and tried to help us. He said some of the same things you are saying, but I kicked him out of the house because I didn't think he knew what he was talking about. How could he know how we felt? He hadn't lost his daughter."

Then she said something I will never forget. "It's different coming from you. You've been there." Right before my very eyes was a demonstration of the lesson I was learning about God's purpose for my pain—that with the same help He had given me I might help others. It was the first of many such experiences that would come my way.

On November 14, 1971, a young woman kissed her husband goodbye, walked out of their Edmonton apartment and right out of his life, without a trace of her whereabouts. Her distraught young husband was to be the next troubled person to enter my life. When the news of Gail McCarthy's disappearance broke, many people began to fear that all three disappearances might be connected. Was there indeed a maniac killer on the loose?

That evening, Gord Sinclair, the **Journal** reporter

who had written the story, called and asked if I would go to see Ian McCarthy. "You have just recently gone through a similar experience and I thought possibly you could be of some help to him. He is completely strung out."

I expressed my immediate hesitation. "But I don't even know the man," I said. "He probably won't want to see me." Mr. Sinclair, however, was persistent. I agreed to call Ian McCarthy and if he wished to talk to me I would go to see him. When I called he was understandably edgy until I explained who I was. Then I thought he sounded somewhat pleased that I would come.

He is a tall, thin man, and after four days of desperate frustration, he looked even thinner. His face was pale and drawn. At first we didn't talk much. We just sat in the same room and shared an experience that words couldn't adequately describe. I asked a few questions, hoping he would begin to talk.

Then, over a cup of coffee which he poured with trembling hands, he shared his feelings. I knew somewhat how he felt. I knew something of what he was going through and I just let him talk. He had slept only two hours in nearly four days. He had done almost everything he could think of by himself and in cooperation with the police to solve the mystery. They had been happily married and he could think of no reason why she would just walk out on him, nor could he think of any motive why anyone would want to hurt her. She was generally a kind and gentle person and they had just recently shared the good news that she was expecting her first baby. He was understandably bitter, and I well knew the feeling of frustration which comes after having tried everything possible without success.

When he had finished talking, I began to share

some of my own experience. In particular, I wanted him to know my source of strength and help. I told him how I had come to depend even more upon God and His Word as my constant source of help. I sought to infuse some measure of strength and courage into him in the same manner in which I had received it myself. Yet, when I left him later that evening, I really wondered if I had been able to help him at all. I learned later through friends that he later stated in a radio interview that after I had left he had done something which he had never done before in his life. He had knelt down by his bed and prayed for strength and help.

We met again on a number of occasions and experienced a bond that we could not express in words. We were just two young men suffering through a similar experience. I have since lost contact with him, but still think of him often. If in some way I was able to pass on some help to him I am glad. I am happy to have been of help and I am happy for any good that came from my own suffering.

As time went on I became more and more aware of just how keen the interest was in our case. I received assurances of prayerful concern from numerous churches and individuals from many parts of the world and I sensed deeply the effect of their support.

Many were most anxious to do whatever they could to help in any way possible. One night early in January I answered the phone just as I was leaving the house. It was from a Vancouver radio station asking me if I would be willing to join them on their "Nightline," live, via long-distance telephone. It was a privilege for me to talk to Mike Dixon of CJOR in Vancouver and share with his listeners my personal feelings and my confidence that God had everything well in hand and that I expected Him to

87

work it out in His own time and way. Once again the purpose of my suffering took on a new meaning as the circle of influence widened.

However, perhaps the most important and far-reaching experience came on Christmas day, 1971. With the two boys, I travelled to Calgary to be with members of my family, who, needless to say, shared my deep hurt in many ways that only family members can. We sat in the living room in the home of my youngest brother, Henry, and his wife, Nettie. There was no generation gap as we sat, adults and teenagers together, and sensed that our family, which was never really closely knit, was being drawn together in a new way.

They were, of course, keenly interested in all that had transpired and so I sat and shared with them step by step how I had learned to draw upon the limitless grace of God for strength and courage in every new aspect of my life. We began early in the afternoon and time was forgotten as others in turn shared how their lives had been affected by the experience. Finally, late that evening, we decided to spend some time together praying for each other and for our circumstances as a whole. Once again it was during such a time that God implanted within my heart and mind a thought which further extended my contact with people who needed help.

When we concluded our prayer session I rather hesitantly commented about my thoughts. "Somehow I feel I ought to share some of these things with some of the churches which have stood by me so faithfully in prayer." I was hesitant because I didn't want to seem presumptuous or sensational, but I felt a strong impression that that was what I should do.

John Siemens, my brother-in-law, immediately concurred with me. He said, "You know, I was just sitting here thinking that our church people would

want to hear you share these victories with them."
That started the ball rolling in a new and exciting
direction.

I determined one thing right away. I would go only
where I was asked to go—I would never actively seek
an invitation anywhere. But wherever the invitations
were forthcoming, I would do everything physically
possible to accept each one. God knew best where
He wanted me to share the victories for His glory.

So it was that on January 23, 1972 I stood on the
platform of the Highlands Mennonite Brethren
Church in Calgary, Alberta and for the first time
during a church service shared my experiences. I
would share them in many other places in the
following months, each appointment arranged
without any manipulation on my part. I believe they
were divinely arranged because of what happened as
a result.

Before I share the wonderful stories of those
meetings, let me touch on one other thing first. I was
deeply concerned that wherever I went, I would not
draw attention to myself, but rather draw attention
to the wonderful grace of God. As I shared that with
my loving Lord one morning in my quiet moments
with Him, He once again spoke through the pages of
His Word in a very simple manner, yet His message
was so unmistakably clear:

"Yet we who have this spiritual treasure are like
common clay pots to show that the supreme power
belongs to God, not to us. We are often troubled, but
not crushed; sometimes in doubt, but never in
despair; there are enemies, but we are never without
a friend; and though badly hurt at times, we are not
destroyed. At all times we carry in our mortal bodies
the death of Jesus so that His life also may be seen in
us" (II Corinthians 4:7-10).

It was an insight which certainly stood me in good stead. God's purpose in my suffering was that He might have a simple-but-living means of displaying His love, His concern, His tender compassion, His power, and His glory. He did not want anything to detract in any way from what He was trying to accomplish. So He chose insignificant and unknown little me as a "common clay pot" to demonstrate by living example how He is able to intervene in the life of any individual who will trust Him. The more common and ordinary the vessel, the more attention is given to the treasure, and so, as I travelled about, it was my sole desire to let the life of Jesus be seen in me.

The one interesting and wonderful thing that emerged from that venture in Calgary was simply this. God arranged about ten such opportunities to share with large and small groups what He had done for me. In each place there was always some evidence of the reason for the appointment. There were always one or more persons present who needed especially to hear me share my experiences because of specific needs in their own lives. At each meeting there were one or two that came to my attention, but I firmly believe that much more was accomplished, but without my knowledge, so as to insure that I would not become proud, but continue as a simple, ordinary, common, clay pot.

In Calgary, in the Mennonite Church I referred to earlier, it was a young lady who had been widowed a few years before in a very trying ordeal. She spoke to me in person and I heard later from another source how her life had been affected by hearing how God had intervened in my life.

In Medicine Hat, Alberta, on February 11, 1972, it was my privilege to speak to about 350 people at a "Sweethearts' Banquet" sponsored by the Medicine

Hat Christian Women's Club. It was "Men's Night," so each lady had been encouraged to bring her husband or escort to the Columbia Club at 350 First Avenue N.E. I remember thinking that I must have been the only one there that night without an escort. But by that time I was becoming completely engrossed in the joy of being able to help others.

I remarked that night to Alan Reynar, who was sitting next to me, that I had stopped begging God to end my ordeal. I was completely content to say, "Lord, first fulfill all of Your purposes, and then I know You will end the uncertainty under which we struggle." That night, because I was so far away from the piano, I rather blew my attempt at singing. Just another reminder, I think, of the fact that I was only the clay pot. But the Lord just sort of turned me loose that night as I shared some of the truths which lead to victorious living in the midst of trial. I felt completely at ease and sensed that the Lord was moving in many lives.

Why did God arrange to have me there that night? There was a couple there who had lost their daughter in a tragic accident, and they were groping for answers. There was a man there suffering from a rare and fatal nerve disease. He knew he was slowly but surely dying. That contact was one among many other contacts that helped him to accept his condition so he himself could influence others. He spoke to me afterward and shared with me how he had absorbed some of the strength and courage I had received and was passing on to him. He died shortly after that, a victorious person.

And so it went. In one meeting it was a teenage girl with deep-seated problems at home. As she saw the treasure of God's glory in this clay pot, she reached out and experienced an infusion of strength and courage to bear her own burdens. In other

91

meetings a young man with a persistent question on his mind found what he sought as he saw a living demonstration of what God can do in and with an ordinary, common person.

Then the Lord arranged a church meeting where I was to encounter Him in a new way. I was the one who came with the need that was to be met. The Lendrum Mennonite Brethren Church was without a minister and a very good friend of mine called and asked if I would bring the morning message on Easter Sunday. We had known each other as kids living on neighboring farms. Now, in another setting many years later, Dr. George Loewen called and asked me to address the congregation of his church.

I emphasized two main facts that morning. First, that the Resurrection of Jesus Christ from the dead is the very foundation of our faith. "And if Christ has not been raised, then your faith is a delusion and you are lost in your sins..." (I Corinthians 15:17). Second, that the Resurrection of Christ is the guarantee of our own resurrection from the dead. "But the truth is that Christ has been raised from death, as the guarantee that those who sleep in death will also be raised" (I Corinthians 15:20).

It was then that I referred to the beautiful passage that God was to use to meet my need that day. Jesus stood before the tomb of His very dear friend named Lazarus, whose sisters, Mary and Martha, were mourning his untimely passing. In His encounter with Mary and Martha, Jesus uttered what to me are the most thrilling words in all of the Bible: "I am the Resurrection and the Life. Whoever believes in me will live, even though he dies; and whoever lives and believes in me will never die. Do you believe this?" (John 11:25,26).

As I read that passage to the congregation that morning I sensed that it was being divinely directed right at me. The question burned in my heart—"Do you believe this?" I found myself responding as Martha had, with a resounding, "Yes, Lord! I do believe...."

My soul filled with new hope as I saw as I had never seen before that death is not the end. The grave is merely the doorway to a new and glorious life for those whose faith rests upon the finished work of Christ on Calvary. As I look back I see how God used that encounter to infuse into me new strength and courage for the new ordeal that lay just two weeks down the road.

As I moved through my appointments during those winter months I used to sing two songs. I would begin with a song entitled, "He Giveth More Grace." The words by Annie Johnson Flint were put to music by Herbert Mitchel:

He giveth more grace when the burdens grow greater,
He sendeth more strength as the labors increase.
To added affliction He addeth his mercy
To multiplied trials, His multiplied peace.

Chorus:
His love has no limit, His grace has no measure,
His power has no boundary known unto men.
For out of His infinite riches in Jesus
He giveth and giveth and giveth again.

When we have exhausted our store of endurance,
When our strength has failed, ere the day is half done,
When we've reached the end of our hoarded

resources
Our Father's full giving is only begun.

I used to begin with that song to set the stage for demonstrating from my own experience the sufficiency of the wonderful grace of God, if we will only learn to draw daily for each need.

The other song, which I used to sing to end my presentation, simply reminds us of the brevity of this life and the importance of living our lives for His glory at all times. The words by Virgil P. Brock remind us very solemnly of our precarious tenure here and urge us to use for God and to the best advantage each moment we have.

Today is mine, tomorrow may not come
I may not see the rising of the sun.
When evening falls, my work may all be done
Today is mine, tomorrow may not come.

Today is mine, to sing a joyful song,
Its notes may cheer some wanderer in the throng,
His steps may falter, while my own are strong
Today is mine to sing a joyful song.

Today is mine to do a loving deed.
A burden lift from one who is in need.
To help some soul, I'll go with joy and speed
Today is mine to do a loving deed.

Today is mine, tomorrow may not come
My race of life may end at set of sun,
Shall I then hear my Master say, "Well done"
Today is mine, tomorrow may not come. [5]

The words almost seemed like a voice from the

past, a voice from heaven. When September 15, 1971 had dawned, none of us (and certainly not MaryAnn) had expected that before the sun would set, MaryAnn's "race of life" would end, and yet it had. It served as a powerful reminder to all of us to use each moment as if it were our last.

As I relate these insights into the reasons why God allows His own to suffer so deeply at times, it is my deep desire that this book will serve as another means of broadening the scope of help that God intended from the sharing of my experience. It is my hope and prayer that others who have deep troubles of all kinds will find through the reading of these pages an infusion of strength that will give them steel in their spines and starch in their muscles so that they will be able to bear the load. It is not enough merely to endure. God intends for us to draw upon the unlimited resources of His grace, not only to endure, but to live in glorious victory.

Some people, with good intentions I'm sure, have suggested that I must be a special person to have been entrusted with such a deep trial. I have always vigorously opposed that suggestion, stating that God can do exactly the same for any individual as He did for me. We only have to yield to His will and learn each day to draw enough strength to meet each burden. I am only the clay pot that God chose in this instance to display His glorious treasure.

These insights God saw fit to let me see. I believe there are many more factors which we cannot see now. Today, as we look at the pattern of our lives being woven on God's loom, we see it from the back side. We see many knots and loose ends with only a dim outline of the picture. Some day, when all the weaving is complete, we will view it from the right side. We will see the wonderful purposes in total and then the whole pattern will make glorious sense. Till then, we accept by faith what now we cannot yet fully understand.

1 From **Knowing God's Secrets**, by John E. Hunter, Copyright 1965 by Zondervan Publishing House. Used by permission.
2 Ibid., p. 93
3 Ibid., p. 89
4 Ibid., p. 89
5 "Today is Mine," Composer: Blanche Kerr Brock, Author: Virgil P. Brock, Copyright 1941 by The Rodeheaver Co., Owner International copyright secured. Used by permission.

V
MORE SINISTER SHADOWS

Whenever a person steps suddenly from bright light into a deep shadow it takes time for his eyes to become adjusted. But in time, as his eyes become accustomed to the darkness, the shadow no longer holds the dread it did before. Objects which at first were totally hidden by the impenetrable shadows begin to take shape again.

When on September 15, 1971 I stepped into the dark shadows that were to be a part of my life for many months, it was as though my mind were blinded by the sudden darkness that surrounded me. I was confused and bewildered by my sudden loss. I was frustrated beyond description by the fact that we did not know what had happened and could do nothing about it. I was afraid to face whatever the future might hold. Nevertheless, with the passing of time, I became somewhat adjusted to the circumstances and life again took on some form of routine.

But as I gradually adjusted to the gloomy shadows, I became aware that there were more sinister shadows lurking ominously in the background. Very quickly these moved into the foreground and played a prominent role in the whole ordeal.

It all began one day shortly after MaryAnn's disappearance. I was sitting in the homicide division of the city police department across the desk from

Detective Gowler. We were discussing the many aspects of the case when suddenly he alerted me to an aspect I had not considered. He warned me to be prepared for what are commonly called "crank calls." These calls come mainly from the "lunatic fringe." I had no previous experience with them, but judging by what I had heard from others, they were a rather unnerving prospect.

I got my first such call about two days later. The male voice, rather blurry and slow, almost unintelligibly mumbled something about me, about MaryAnn, and about how he was sorry for what had happened. Possibly that first call was well-intentioned, but not so some of the others.

It was only the beginning. I learned that what was so new to me was "old hat" to the police. Apparently, crank calls happen all the time and add an additional load to an already overburdened police department. From the volume of incoming information, the police could easily spend most of their time chasing some people's lunatic dreams.

Let me share an example with you. One Saturday evening I answered the telephone to hear a male voice say, "Mr. Plett?"

"Yes, who is calling, please?"

"That doesn't really matter."

"I always like to know," I said.

"I won't give you my name, but I can tell you where your wife is."

Naturally, by then I was keenly interested, but I also wanted to be cautious. "Oh, how do you know?" I said. "Have you called the police?"

During our twenty-minute conversation this is what he told me: He could tell me where MaryAnn was and what had happened to her. He had had a dream in which he had seen her very clearly. (That was strange since he had never seen her before in person, although he had seen her picture in the paper.) From his dream he knew that she had been stabbed to death. By using some mysterious method, which he said he could not explain over the phone, he stated that he had determined that her body was buried somewhere southwest of Cooking Lake. If I would come to his apartment, and he gave me his address, he would show me his sure-fire method.

I said, "Man, if you think I'm going out alone after dark to meet you in your apartment so you can tell me how you know where my wife's body is buried—either you're crazy, or you think I am!"

I was still fishing for some clue that might tell me more about him, when he suddenly stopped talking, but did not hang up the receiver. Since he had originated the call, my phone was tied up until he hung up. Since he did not hang up, I figured that he didn't want me to call the police. I ran next door to the neighbors to use their phone and learned that the police already knew about it.

The man had called me from a public phone in the Saxony Hotel. Some alert person had overheard him talking, and upon hearing the nature of the conversation, had used another phone to call the police. They picked him up within minutes.

Just what was the great method he had been telling me about? He had taken a highway map, a piece of string, and his ring. With the ring hanging on the string, he had waved it over the map until he had been able to "feel the vibrations," which then had told him where she was located. Needless to say, he was wrong in his prediction, but whether sincere or not, he had merely added to my distress and certainly added to the police work load.

Even more disturbing to me were calls from people who were involved with mediums, clairvoyants, and fortune-tellers. Let me state clearly right here that while I do not deny that there is some "power" operating in these people which may occasionally enable them to be right, it is my firm conviction that that power is not the divine Power Who was the Source of my strength and confidence during those difficult months.

I stated this very forcefully one day to a woman on the telephone. She was one of several who kept calling, suggesting that I contact a clairvoyant. I kept putting her off until one day she called to inform me that she had made two long-distance calls to Ontario to arrange an appointment for me. It was time to state my conviction clearly.

"Lady," I said, "as far as I am concerned, I want nothing to do with you or your kind. I believe that you and I are on opposite sides, serving different masters. As far as the mystery of MaryAnn's whereabouts is concerned, I have complete confidence that when God is ready, He will reveal it without your help. Until then, I do not want to know." I guess she understood because she did not call again.

But with her call, a new insight began to crystallize in my mind. I began to see the whole experience as a contest between God and the devil. I had publicly declared my confidence in God's goodness and wisdom. I believed that God had allowed the abduction for a purpose and that part of that purpose was that He would be glorified in the outcome. I believed that He was in full control at all times.

I had publicly gone out on a limb with God. As a result, God's honor was at stake, and when it comes to His honor He leaves no doubt about His position. He says: "I am the Lord; that is my name and my glory I will not give to another, nor my praise to graven images" (Isaiah 42:8, Amplified). We know

100

from the Scriptures that there is a devil and that he is totally contrary to God and all that is good. He would have liked nothing better than to trap me into a position of compromise. Just suppose that a clairvoyant had successfully led me to MaryAnn. Then when people asked, "How did you find her?" I would have had to reply, "Well, I went to a clairvoyant and found the answer."

But I was not about to become trapped in a compromise. I am convinced that when confronted with implicit trust in God, clairvoyants and their kind cannot perform successfully. I said publicly on a number of occasions that I had come to view the whole experience as a contest between God and Satan and that I was sure that when all the facts were revealed God would get the glory. I was sure that all the predictions made about the case would be proven wrong, and they were. To me, it is a glorious triumph of faith that God vindicated His name. When I put Him on the spot, as it were, and openly declared my confidence in Him, I came into contact with so many different groups and types of mystics that for the sake of simplicity, I have lumped them all together under one term: the occult. To me, they all belong in the same category because they are all contrary to God.

Let me give you a prime example. On November 11, 1971, when my interview with Jim Roberts was aired over CFRN radio, there was also an interview with Paul Napora, who claimed certain powers to predict future events. At first the knowledge that he would appear on the same program bothered me. I was afraid that people might think we had something in common. But when I heard what he had to say, I knew I had no reason to be concerned. I was reminded of the biblical account of Balaam and how God had made a donkey speak in order to fulfill His purposes. I remember commenting to friends on several occasions, "Let this man shoot off his mouth on the air. When the results are tabulated, he will be proven totally wrong." He was.

Here is the unedited text of the Napora interview as it pertained to MaryAnn, along with the actual facts of the case as we know them:

Question:

Have you received any symbolisms as to the whereabouts of Mrs. Plett?

Answer:

Yes, I have—I have got the strongest belief that she's very much alive and one of the first signs I got was that she—they were in Calgary and from Calgary to Vancouver. I do get her in the B.C. area and she's very much alive—is one of the symbolisms I get.

The fact is that she died on September 15, 1971. Her death certificate states that and all other evidence points to it. I saw someone driving her car late that same night. When the car was later found, her wig, and several stains of her blood type were found in the trunk. So she could not very well have been in "the B.C. area very much alive" on November 11, 1971. It is also very interesting to me that he said "they" were travelling, as though she were travelling voluntarily. No one who knew her well ever believed for a moment that she would leave of her own choice.

Question:

Has there been any word to anybody since her disappearance?

Answer:

Not to my knowledge, at least they're not coming out with any statement to that effect. I don't believe that she's communicating at this particular time, but I do believe that her husband will hear from her about the third week of March in 1972—is one of the beliefs I do have. One of the symbolisms I did get even this morning is that she did make a phone call to someone but to whom I couldn't tell you—this is something I do not know but that is the symbolism I got when I got up this morning. I did some deep meditation on her. To me it's an undercurrent—I get an undercurrent and that's about all I can say.

The fact very simply is that since she was no longer living it was impossible for her to have made the phone call to which he refers. There was no phone call. Another fact is that no one, not even her husband, heard from her on the third week of March 1972.

I remember that I had hopes of her being found during every week of those seven long months, except that third week of March. Somehow I was sure, and declared it publicly at that time, that in no way would God allow His honor to be given to another by MaryAnn's return during that week. I understand that in a subsequent interview with Jim Roberts on March 17, 1972, Mr. Napora extended his prediction by about two weeks. Again he was very wrong. God allowed the discovery of the body to come two weeks after the time designated in Napora's second, updated prediction—just to make sure that no one would be able to rob Him of His honour. In my mind, Mr. Napora's reference of an "undercurrent" is evidence that because of my implicit trust in God, he was being thwarted by powers higher than his own sources.

Question:

Her briefcase was found eighty miles northwest of the city—have you been able to tie that in at all?

Answer:

That again to me is deception. I get the feeling of deception and the particular gentleman that was with her would not gain by her death and I did not see her in the spirit, so I do get that she is very, very much alive. She certainly is not passed over.

The facts once again contradict his statements. The discovery of the briefcase proved to be the very thing that later led to the discovery of her body. Everyone in that area was alert to the possibility that her body may have been disposed of near there, so that when workmen found articles of her clothing the following spring it was only natural that they would report the find to the Royal Canadian Mounted Police. When the police arrived at that spot with their tracking dog it was only a matter of time till her remains were discovered. Mr Napora's insistence on November 11 that she was "very, very much alive" and that she was certainly "not passed over" only serves to prove again how wrong he was.

Question:

So there would be nothing to tie in with the blood that was found in the back seat of the car in the car lot?

Answer:

Again too that blood sample I don't believe was her blood. I don't believe that there was any connection and that that was her blood at all. So I do not for one moment see her passed over. I would have seen her in spirit by now and I've done some very, very deep meditation on this and of course my guide told me that she is very much alive as well. So I have got to go by that—I've got to go by that statement. I know even when I go into missing animals or missing people, I will know if they are passed over and she is not one of them. She is very much alive.

There is an error here in the question. The blood stains were found in the trunk of the car, not on the back seat. The blood typing done by the city police lab technician proved without doubt that the blood was of her type. That, coupled with the obvious fact that her body had been in the trunk, gives the lie to his assertion that it was not her blood.

Again, as you can see, he insisted that she had "not passed over," meaning of course that she was alive at that point. His information, coming from his "guide," as he called him, whoever that may be, indicates that his guide was also unable to ascertain the truth. He admitted that he had not been able to see her in spirit. In other words, he had not been able to identify her in the realm of the dead, nor make any sort of contact that might identify her.

I am convinced that the reason he could not see her in spirit, in spite of all his deep meditation, was that because MaryAnn had committed herself to the Lord in life, her spirit had not gone to the realm of those who die without faith in Christ. Since Mr. Napora's guide obviously was limited to the realm of the unbelieving dead, there could be no contact at all.

The apostle Paul declared: "So we are always full of courage. We know that as long as we are at home

105

in this body we are away from the Lord's home. For our life is a matter of faith, not of sight. We are full of courage and would much prefer to leave our home in this body and be at home with the Lord. More than anything else, however, we want to please Him, whether in our home here or there'' (II Corinthians 5:6-9).

In another letter, Paul stated: "I am caught from both sides: I want very much to leave this life and be with Christ, which is a far better thing; but it is more important, for your sake, that I remain alive" (Philippians 1:23,24).

These verses clearly show that the person who dies believing in Christ is ushered directly into that heavenly realm where God the Father and Jesus reside. So all the while that Mr. Napora and his guide were seeking MaryAnn's spirit, MaryAnn was safely home rejoicing in the indescribable beauty and glory of her wonderful Saviour. No amount of meditation will enable any living person to cross the fixed boundary of that realm. So, even though her body was lifeless (contrary to what Mr. Napora said), her soul and spirit are very much alive in heaven today.

Question:
    Will the police find her or will it be her appearance will come about because she phones Mr. Plett?

Answer:
    Yes, I believe that her appearance will come by herself. I do not believe that the police will really have to find her. I feel that she will come around on her own volition. I don't feel that it will be necessary—I know that there will be contact. There will definitely be contact.

Once again, the facts speak for themselves.

Her appearance could not and did not come by herself, because only her lifeless remains were left on earth. The police did have to take their tracking dog and locate her body in the dense brush near Fort Assiniboine. And once again there definitely could not be, nor was there, any contact with her whatever.

In that same interview, Napora also talked about the Armstrong case. It is not necessary to quote verbatim what he said, because it is so very repetitious. But he was asked eight questions in all and to five of these he gave essentially the same answer:

> I do believe implicitly that these people have disappeared into the fourth dimension—in other words, they have just slipped right over in the flesh. This is my belief of the Armstrong people—that they have slipped into the fourth dimension.

He admitted that the Armstrong car would have had to slip over into the "fourth dimension" with them. That is very interesting since he first tried to describe the "fourth dimension" as a house and later said, "It's as if they become air." It is also interesting to me that he apparently never tried to see their spirits or make contact with them, in the light of the fact that we now know that they perished in a pond on the night of September 4, 1971. I believe the facts speak for themselves. God has vindicated His name and proven that He alone can be trusted implicitly.

The Scriptures are abundantly clear on this subject of the various cults and the occult. First of all, let us consider a very general statement made by Jesus Himself when He was confronted by the religious rulers of His day: "Anyone who is not for me is really against me; anyone who does not help me gather is really scattering" (Matthew 12:30).

Jesus stated a very basic principle. Anyone who assumes for himself the right to make predictions about the future, who claims special knowledge, or who claims to possess supernatural powers—unless that person is openly committed to serve Jesus Christ, he is in actuality against him. There can be no neutral position. Such a person is either for Christ or against Christ. He is either helping or hurting His cause.

There may be instances when someone has displayed supernatural ability. Someone's predictions may have been reasonably accurate. Maybe someone does possess powers of such unusual perception that some people are persuaded to believe in these powers. But these things do not alter the principle—unless such people are openly committed **to** Christ they are **against** Him.

For example, in the biblical record of Exodus when Moses was sent to Pharaoh to plead for the deliverance of Israel, God used Moses as His human instrument to bring about certain supernatural happenings. Pharaoh countered with his own sorcerers, who were able to duplicate the first three of those happenings. But they failed on all the rest. So I am not denying that there may be certain powers vested in leaders and members of the occult, but these powers cannot come from God.

Saint Paul touched on another principle which is important for us to notice. He wrote to Timothy about certain people who were offering false teachings to people who through lack of training still could not distinguish between truth and error. He said to them: "They want to be teachers of God's law, but they do not understand their own words or the matters about which they speak with so much confidence" (I Timothy 1:7). The principle is clear.

Those involved in cults and the occult, whether leaders or followers, **may** be completely sincere in what they believe or teach, but be sincerely wrong.

Truth gets confused with error. Fantasy is confused with reality. Imagination is mistaken for inspiration. Volumes of words are mistaken for wisdom. What is weird and spooky is considered wonderful and profound. Sincerely desiring truth—but having forsaken its source, the Holy Scriptures—these people often find themselves trapped in a festival of ceremonies that leave them no choice but to stumble farther and farther down the dark and gloomy path of the unknown, until, blinded by the devil himself, they actually begin to worship him. No measure of sincerity will ever safeguard them against the devil's deceptions.

Let me take this a step farther. We are told in Scripture: "Do not defile yourselves by consulting mediums and wizards, for I am Jehovah your God" (Leviticus 19:31, LB). The principle again is clearly stated. Involvement in the occult has a defiling effect on the participant's mind and, indeed, on his whole inner being. Once this happens, he readily begins to call "black" that which is "white," and "white" that which is "black." Truth becomes error, and error, truth. Good becomes evil, and evil, good. What began as speculation takes on the nature of truth and reality.

What he does not realize is that once he is defiled by such contacts, he can easily become a slave to the desires and passions dictated by his own fallen human nature. His defiled nature expresses itself in actions contrary to God's moral law, which is clearly expressed in His Word. Plagued by the knowledge that he has transgressed that law, he is driven on to become involved in such a degrading activity as what we've read about it recent headlines—the sacrificing of human lives in order to appease Satan, the object of occult worship. While many never reach the ultimate degredation of outright demon worship, the occult is nonetheless a slippery and dangerous path to travel.

God says: "I will set my face against anyone who consults mediums and wizards instead of me and I will cut that person off from his people" (Leviticus 20:6, LB). In the history of Israel recorded in Scripture, we are told of a king of Israel who slipped to the very depths of evil as he followed the treacherous trail of the occult. Here is the record: "...Manasseh sacrificed his own children as burnt offerings in the Valley of Hinnom. He consulted spirit-mediums, too, and fortune-tellers and sorcerers and encouraged every sort of evil, making the Lord very angry" (II Chronicles 33:6, LB). This illustrates the capacity for evil latent in human nature and reminds us again how dangerous it is to follow the slippery downgrade of the occult. While the penalty for such involvement may be delayed so that it does not even occur in this life, it does not alter the fact that God's anger will result in the judgment of those who are guilty.

One might well ask the occultists, then, the same questions the prophet Isaiah asked Israel many hundreds of years ago: "So why are you trying to find out the future by consulting witches and mediums? Don't listen to their whisperings and mutterings. Can the living find out the future from the dead? Why not ask your God? Check these witches' words against the Word of God! He says, 'If their messages are different from mine, it is because I have not sent them; for they have no light or truth in them' " (Isaiah 8:19,20, LB). Had the Israeli people followed God's revealed truth in the first place, they would not have needed to seek for answers elsewhere and would not have become enmeshed in the devil's trap.

In the light of what we have said, one might wonder, "How can I know who is of God and what is of God?" The answer is very revealing in the light of the interview I have recorded in this chapter. God, speaking to His people, stated: "If you wonder, 'how shall we know if the prophecy is from the Lord or not?' this is the way to know: If the thing he prophesies doesn't happen, it is not the Lord who has given him the message; he has made it up himself. You have nothing to fear from him" (Deuteronomy 18:21,22, LB). The criterion which God has laid down as a test for His prophets is one hundred percent accuracy one hundred percent of the time. There is no room for even the slightest margin of error when God has given the message.

I am convinced that when occultists are confronted by a person who displays implicit trust in God, they cannot be successful because then God's honor is involved, and He will not give that to anyone else.

As I look back now and see how sinister the shadows I faced were, and remember how distressed I was at the time, how glad I am that I did not compromise my faith in any way. I am deeply grateful to God that He gave me the grace and courage to stand firmly by the convictions that I knew were right.

The shadows were long, dark, and sinister, but by the grace of God I was enabled to walk without fear in the full and glorious confidence that God had everything under control. After all, His honor was at stake. I had gone out on a limb with Him, remember? Well, that proved to be the safest place I could be!

VI

WHO CAST THE SHADOWS?

On a blistering day a shadow can bring welcome relief from the blazing sun. But on a day when brisk, fall winds keep the temperature near the freezing point in spite of the sunshine, the shadow of a cloud hiding the face of the sun can make a person button up his coat a little tighter to keep the shivers from playing tag on his spine. A quick glance at the sky will suffice to answer the query, "What caused the shadow?"

When on September 15, 1971 we were engulfed in the chilling shadows of personal tragedy caused by MaryAnn's mysterious disappearance, all of us were asking the following questions: "Who?", "Who was 'Cooper?' Who was responsible for MaryAnn's disappearance?"

This chapter will give some insight into the work of the police, whose job it is to discover the answers. Both the Edmonton City Police, under the capable direction of Staff Sergeant Poss and Detective Al Gowler, and Corporal Hatch of the local Royal Canadian Mounted Police detachment conducted intensive but inconclusive investigations. So far, they have been stymied in all their attempts to locate the client MaryAnn took to the acreage on that fateful day. We are still asking the question, "Who cast the shadow?"

I have stated earlier my conviction that God first of

all gave His consent in the courts of heaven before the abduction occurred. I have stated my firm belief that at all times He was in complete control of all events. The man, whose alias was James Cooper, was merely the human instrument through whom the whole case was triggered. By that I do not mean that he was a victim of his fate and could not help doing what he did. He was not a robot acting on the impulse signals of a computer. Instead, he was a man with perfect freedom of choice either to commit or not to commit the heinous crime. He chose to do it and so he became the object of one of the most intensive manhunts in Alberta since the search for Frank Wiley, the missing golf pro who disappeared from the city of Edmonton on April 19, 1962.

Our fine police forces work hard to protect you and me, yet often come in for more than their share of criticism. True, they sometimes make mistakes because they are human, but they deserve all the support we can give them. I am convinced, after having seen something of the intensive efforts of the combined police forces, that in our case everything was done that was humanly possible to do. I have no complaints about the way the case was handled.

During those first two weeks, I went to the city police station almost every day for one reason or another. I asked questions when I didn't undersand why they did certain things in a certain way. I suggested things that I thought they might have somehow overlooked. They always answered my questions as best as they could and treated every scrap of information as though it were vital evidence. Many times I began with the words, "You know, this may sound stupid, but I've been wondering if...." And then came another of my classic suggestions. Occasionally they immediately discounted my ideas and stated their reasons clearly. On a few occasions, however, I managed to make suggestions which made them raise their eyebrows and say, "That is a possibility. We will check it out."

The city police force worked side-by-side with the R.C.M.P. in the investigation. The R.C.M.P. were involved from the beginning because there were indications that the crime had been committed outside the city, placing the case under their jurisdiction. Because the car was found in the city, the city police were also involved. Then, too, with the public interest that was generated by the various media, the two forces had to work together to check out all the leads within their own jurisdictions. Certainly in all of the instances with which I am familiar, there was excellent cooperation between the two forces.

I believe that they did a very thorough and professional job, which unfortunately has not been enough to close the case successfully, at least up to the time of this writing. However, I am still confident that the moment will come when I will hear them say to me, "We have apprehended the man who murdered your wife." Then we will be able to say, "There is the man who cast the shadows over our lives."

While the family was hoping against hope that MaryAnn might still be found alive, particularly in the beginning, both Corporal Hatch and Detective Gowler told me, after her body was discovered, that they had treated the case as homicide from the very beginning. Detective Gowler, who has since been promoted to sergeant, stated that when the report first came to him it was as a request for "assistance to locate" a missing person. From his past experience, which is considerable, he began to think in terms of homicide as the details of the disappearance became clearer. When the car was found two days later, the evidence it provided left very little doubt in his mind that it could be anything but homicide. They were professionals working on a case. I was family, very much emotionally involved, fearing the worst while hoping for the best.

The first request for an "assist to locate" was made by Graham Realty at 8:08 P.M. on Wednesday, September 15, 1971. But it wasn't until I spotted MaryAnn's car around 11:00 P.M. that night that things really began to happen. Detectives Brian Scott and Cliff Tetslaff were on their way to the Real Estate office when we all gave chase after MaryAnn's car, which had just then cruised right by the office. Within minutes police radios all over the city crackled with an all-points bulletin: "Watch for a 1970 two-tone-green Pontiac Laurentian bearing Alberta licence number LN 54-07." As far as we can determine now, however, the car had already been parked by that time and so was off the streets. Once Cooper had left the car, he was clear. No one was able to tie him to the crime.

Meanwhile, I had gone home and shortly thereafter Detectives Scott and Tetslaff were at my house gathering more firsthand information. In Chapter Two I described how Mrs. Cote and I went with these two detectives, along with one of the city police dogs and his handler, to the acreage late that night. We were met there by Corporal Bill Stroud of the Leduc, Alberta, R.C.M.P. detachment, since the acreage was under their jurisdiction. We searched until morning.

After that the activity became very intense. The R.C.M.P. concentrated their efforts at the acreage. During the next few days aircraft and dogs were used to comb the area, with no results. On Monday September 20, thirty-three men from the Canadian Forces Base in Namao, Alberta and sixteen

R.C.M.P. constables did a shoulder-to-shoulder search of the entire acreage. They were thorough, but unsuccessful in finding anything useful to the investigation.

Their efforts then turned to the slough which is located on the acreage near the road. Together with the county fire department they spent about eighteen hours pumping out the water. Then every foot of that slimy slough bottom was probed for clues. As a result of that probe, I developed a greater respect for police thoroughness. Corporal Stroud was in charge of the operation. Early that morning, unknown to any of the men involved in the search, he had taken a paper cup, weighted it with a rock so it would sink, and thrown it in the slough. His men later found the cup down on the muddy bottom and certainly deserved full marks for their efficiency.

Meanwhile, the city police were pressing the investigation within the city. A check of all hotels and motels turned up no less than four men named "Cooper," all of whom were thoroughly checked out. On Thursday and Friday mornings, they conducted a "grid search" of the entire city. As I understand it, every patrolman that went out had to cover his division block-by-block and lane-by-lane to check every property.

The police are reasonably sure that the car was parked on the service lot at Don Wheaton Car Sales from Wednesday night on. It should then have been spotted by the grid search, but one must remember that the car was parked in the far corner behind a row of other vehicles, so it would easily be missed by a patrol going through the lane. It was not visible from the street either because of a high fence.

The car was located at about 1:30 P.M. on Friday by one of the men working at Don Wheaton's. No one

116

could find a work order detailing repairs to be made on it. Only then did they realize that there on their lot was the object of the intensive search. The police were on the scene within minutes. When I arrived, the car was being dusted inside and out for fingerprints. It was photographed from the inside, from the outside, and from underneath. It was towed from the lot to the police station and received a better cleaning job than it had ever had before. Every inch of that car was gone over.

I watched for awhile as the investigator vacuumed a small area, labelled the deposits, and then repeated the process for each small space. The windshield wipers had been left in the "on" position, indicating that it had been raining the last time the car had been driven. That had to be Wednesday night. The radio dial was set for CJCA, which had not been MaryAnn's choice.

The car was completely empty except for a pair of clip-on sunglasses lying on the front seat. They did not belong to either MaryAnn or myself. Even the glove compartment had been emptied. Inside the trunk was MaryAnn's crumpled wig in one corner and a small bloodstain, about the size of a quarter, on a rug we kept there. There was another smudge of blood on the trunk latch and the area around the latch. I watched as the technician scraped the blood into a small container.

They also found some blue fibres in the trunk which were probably from her coat. The wig was established as MaryAnn's by comparing it with a few strands of fibres caught in MaryAnn's wig brush, which I took to the station. There were twigs and grass caught in the undercarriage of the car. But none of the information helped significantly. The soil and grass samples were too common to help pinpoint an area where the car might have been.

Unfortunately, the efforts to obtain fingerprints from the car were not successful either. Nothing of any real value could be found.

The bloodstains proved to be of her type. The lab technician was concerned that the sample was not large enough for him to be able to type it. But with new materials shipped from Ottawa especially for the case, they were successful in determining that it was of her blood type. That was fortunate, because the small sample of blood allowed them only one chance to type it.

I suppose that the nature of the case caused it to generate more public interest than most other cases. While too much public interest can sometimes hinder police activity, they had so little evidence to go by that they felt they needed the involvement of the public, which they felt might have valuable information pertaining to their investigation. They sought and received the full cooperation of the press, radio, and television. Many citizens became involved and volunteered various bits of information. However, not all of it was helpful. Some of the crank calls resulted in hours of extra leg work for the police. But every shred of information which came in was thoroughly checked and re-checked.

For example, one morning as I sat talking with Detective Gowler in his office, he suddenly broke into our conversation and asked, "Where were you the day before MaryAnn disappeared?"

I said, "At the university. Why?"

"Can you verify that?"

"Yes, I can. My first class was at 8:00 on Tuesday morning. I had four one-and-one-half-hour classes in a row. In each class I handed in my course registration card. You can check it out with the university if you like. I spent some time in the bookstore purchasing books, for which I can show

118

the purchase slip. When I got home, Nelson was sitting on the table crying his heart out. He had a loose tooth that had to come out and he wouldn't let his mother touch it. We removed it before supper. After supper we went to Woodward's Northgate, where we bought the boys some clothes for the new school term. I can show you the proofs of purchase if you like. You can also check with my sister-in-law, Olga Sherstan, because we met her in the store and stopped to talk awhile. Why?"

"Oh, I was just wondering. Do you know MaryAnn's whereabouts that day?"

"Yes, I do. She went to the office at about 9:30 and went with other sales people to see several open houses that had just come onto the market that morning. After that she went back to the office and from there home to give the boys their lunch. At about 1:00 P.M. she filled her car with gas at her brother Bill's service station. You can check it out, if you like.

"I also have in my possession three cancelled cheques which indicate that she went from the service station to Sun Appliances and Furniture to pay a bill. She paid another bill at General Carpet and from there she went to the Saveco store to buy Nelson a watch for his birthday. She was at home when Nelson came home from school at 3:30 and they were trying to pull that tooth when I got home. Why?"

Then he told me an interesting story of how police work can be complicated by a rumor.

"Several weeks ago," he said, "someone called to report that on the afternoon prior to the day on which MaryAnn disappeared, they had seen a man behind the wheel of a car parked on the dirt road leading to the acreage. About a quarter of a mile down the road, a young woman was walking alone, crying.

They had stopped to offer help, but she had refused, mumbling something about a personal problem. Their theory was that possibly you and MaryAnn had had a domestic argument.

"We checked it out and were satisfied that it had nothing to do with this case. Now the story has gone full circle and has come back to us again. This time the car is a two-tone-green Pontiac. You were definitely recognized as the driver and the young woman was definitely MaryAnn. I just had to be sure that you could account for your activities that day."

Well, rumors do start and once they start they do grow. Nevertheless, in spite of instances such as these, it was the consensus of Corporal Hatch and Detective Gowler that all the public interest generated by the case was a definite advantage to them in their investigation. The case is still open and occasional bits of information still come to light now and then.

I never asked Detective Gowler if they ever checked out my story, but I have reasons to believe that for a number of months the only moves I made that were not known to the two police forces were when I rolled over in bed. It's part of their job and I was intelligent enough to know that in such cases the husband has to be considered as one of the prime suspects until proven otherwise. The one advantage I had was that I had nothing to hide and could go about my daily activities without looking for any way to cover up my past or present.

One incident which brought this home to me with full impact occurred shortly before Christmas. Detective Gowler called one day and asked if I would consent to take a polygraph test. He had to explain to me that in simple lay terms that is a lie-detector test. I bristled a bit when he first asked me. If I said, "No," they would think I had something to hide. I

120

knew I was innocent, so it seemed like a totally unnecessary request. It loomed before me as a humiliating prospect. But after we had talked awhile, I consented.

"Really, I have nothing to hide, as I'm sure your test will prove."

"We are sure it will too," he said, "but you know how it is. If this case takes time to solve, even years perhaps, facts become dim and distorted. We want to be able to say that we did everything possible, including a thorough investigation of the husband's activities. This polygraph test is a part of that."

Shortly after the new year, I went to the police station prepared to take the test. By that time, while it was still humiliating, it was sort of fun in a way to be able to prove my innocence.

First, I sat in a small office with the operator. Andrews, I think his name was, went over all the questions he would ask me and talked about how I would answer them. I was surprised at his efforts to convince me that he would ask only the questions he had stated. In fact, one of the questions was, "Are you satisfied that these are all the questions I will ask you?" I was sure he would strap me onto the machine and fire others at me. But not so.

He attached his instruments to my waist and my fingers and we were ready.

"Your name is Jake Plett?"

"Yes."

"You live in the city of Edmonton?"

"Yes."

"In the first sixteen years of your life, can you remember ever having deliberately told a lie to hurt someone?"

I wasn't sure. Certainly I had told lies, but generally the lies were designed for my own protection rather than to hurt someone. I answered,

"No." At that point the three pens recording my reaction went wild, flopping vigorously from side to side.

"Did you have anything to do with MaryAnn's disappearance on September 15, 1971?"

"No."

Right on cue the pens settled down into an almost-straight line.

"In the next sixteen years of your life, can you remember ever deliberately telling a lie to hurt someone?"

I reasoned again that I had lied for my own protection rather than to hurt someone. Again I answered, "No," and again came a flurry of activity on the paper.

"On September 15, 1971 were you in any way responsible for MaryAnn's disappearance?"

"No."

Again the pens responded with an almost-straight line.

"Are you satisfied that I will not ask you any questions other than the ones we have discussed?"

"Yes."

There was a break in the action while we both relaxed for a few moments and then we ran through the whole test again. He asked the same questions, I gave the same answers, and we produced the same results. It was therefore with great satisfaction that I heard Andrews say, "Well, I believe you." He challenged me to go home and think about my answers to his questions about lying.

Even yet I have not been able to recall a time when I deliberately lied to hurt someone, but my uncertainty had clearly registered on the machine. That, contrasted immediately with the opposite reaction to the questions about MaryAnn's disappearance, was what he was looking for. To those, I had registered no uncertainty whatsoever. The police could be assured that I was clean.

Those first few weeks of the investigation were a flurry of activity as various bits of information provided leads that had to be checked out. But each led to the same frustrating dead-end. Then came the day that I had hoped would not come. One day about three weeks after the start of the investigation, Detective Gowler said to me, "We are almost at a dead stop." Staff Sergeant Joe Poss commented, "We've gone over everything a dozen-and-a-half times. We're just at a loss. We've got to get a break somewhere."

The public, aroused by reports of the media, and friends of the family did their best to provide this "break" for the police. I am not sure with whom the idea originated, but early in October someone suggested that a search party cover the entire area in and around the acreage. When the idea was presented to us, both Bill Sherstan and I insisted that it be done only if the police would agree. We didn't want a lot of people tramping over the area if we would interfere with police activity. We contacted both police forces, who agreed to the idea, provided they would be in charge of organizing the search. We would find the people who were interested. They would tell us where to go and what to look for.

I called the Real Estate board to inform them that the search would be conducted on Thanksgiving Monday, October 11, 1971. Public announcements were made in a number of churches in the city. On Sunday, October 10th, the following insert appeared in the bulletin of an Evangelical Free Church in Edmonton:

Search:

The directions for the search tomorrow are as follows: Proceed south on Highway 21 from the junction with Highway 14, nine miles. You will then come to a large curve turning east with a sign reading, "Airport Road." Proceed one mile east, then take the first municipal road south, and following it about 3/4 mile you will come to the acreage with the Graham Realty sign on it. Other instructions will be given orally.

We had no way of guessing how many people would respond. On several preceding Saturdays, I had gone with Bill and a few close friends to search likely areas on our own. But an organized search would involve many more people.

Bill and I were the first to arrive on the scene, except for Corporal Stroud and one other officer. They wanted to know how many people to expect. We couldn't tell them, but we didn't have to wait long before we found out. People came from miles around. There were many Real Estate agents. Most of the men from the church were there. Many people I had never met came from many other churches because they were deeply concerned and wanted to do all they could to help.

My relatives came from Calgary, Brooks, Claresholm, and Gem, all in Alberta. Some of them had gotten up long before dawn to do their farm chores and then driven for four and five hours to get there by 9:30. The municipal road from the highway to the acreage was soon jammed solid with cars. No one took an accurate count, but there were at least seventy-five cars, with two or three searchers per car.

Corporal Stroud was prepared for about a dozen. When his hand-drawn route maps were gone he took a grid map and assigned a section of roadway to each carload of searchers. We were to stop at every farmhouse and talk to people, making them aware of what was going on. We were to report to the police anything that seemed strange or unusual to us. We were to be careful about trespassing on private property without the owner's permission.

From the acreage we fanned out like a small army and spent the day talking, looking, probing in every place that seemed a likely spot to hide a crime. We searched abandoned buildings, surprised some people, and stirred up a lot of new interest. The search resulted in a number of new leads, all of which proved to be dead-ends. The search covered about twenty miles in each direction.

I returned that evening a frustrated and dejected man. I hadn't realized how much I had hoped that day would produce some definite results. Another good plan had resulted in nothing positive.

It was about that time that a very good friend of mine, Freda Wiebe, called me on the telephone with another idea designed to produce some new leads. "Would it be possible," she wanted to know, "to mail out a form letter to all the addresses within a fifty-mile radius of the city to make sure that people, especially the rural people, are aware of the situation?"

I didn't know, but agreed to discuss it with the police. Again I didn't want to do anything that would interfere with or jeopardize the work they were doing. Since the proposed project would obviously mean a lot of leg work for them, it was only right to discuss it with them first.

They agreed to the idea, with a few suggestions. They did not want to be burdened with the extra work of distribution. The cost of mailing would be about $600 in addition to the cost of the paper and printing. They also felt that it would be of no use to mail flyers north of the North Saskatchewan River.

125

In order to cross that river, the man would have had to get on one of the main highways, and cross right through the city. They did not feel that he would take such a risk with a body in the trunk.

That was one point on which I disagreed with them. I countered with a question: "Suppose he did all of the things we don't think he would do because he knew we would think that way?" They agreed that it was possible. So we decided to mail the flyers to all rural addresses in an area up to twenty-five miles north and west of the city and fifty miles south and east of the city. By eliminating all the small towns within that area, we cut down on the volume considerably.

When I talked with Mrs. Wiebe again she offered to look after the whole project and mentioned that she knew some friends who would be interested in helping pay the cost. The printing arrangements were made by Wayne Robinson, Vice-President and Manager of Baker Lovdick Ltd., Advertising, Marketing and Public Relations. Mr. Johanson, Sales Manager of Smith, Davidson and Leckie, arranged for his company to donate the paper. The printing was done free of charge by Commercial Bulletin Printers, where Mr. George Smith is the Assistant Manager. I was hesitant to accept all that help as a donation, but was informed by Mrs. Wiebe that there was no other way. The people virtually insisted they be allowed to donate.

The folded flyer was stamped "Of Vital Concern" on the outside and carried the following message:

"Dear Householder:

WE NEED YOUR HELP!

A month has passed since the mysterious disappearance of Mrs. MaryAnn Plett, local Edmonton Real Estate Agent and mother of two.

HAVE YOU DONE YOUR PART? In checking your property and adjoining wasteland, your buildings (particularly those abandoned), and in thinking back to September 15, 1971 as to whether you may have seen:

A. THE CAR:

1970 Pontiac, four-door sedan, metallic-green bottom, dark-green vinyl roof

Please note: The car had been driven over country roads, and grassy and bushy areas.

B. MRS. PLETT:

Height—5 ft. 2 in. Weight—120 pounds. Dark brown hair, just below the ear, wearing glasses. Last seen wearing heavy brown slacks, brightly printed pant top, brown block-heeled shoes, navy-blue coat, and carrying a hand-tooled purse.

Mrs. Plett in good faith and trust was to show a prospective client an acreage twenty-five miles out of the city. She had with her a black, plastic Real Estate notebook, two black looseleaf binders full of listings, and a dark brown attache case.

C. PROSPECTIVE CLIENT:

The mysterious "Mr. Cooper" has been described as a rather large man and quite a talker. Supposedly he was from Winnipeg, in Edmonton on business.

Items in the car: one white Sunbeam electric can-opener; two pairs of clip-on sunglasses in brown cases; one box Kleenex; one green-blue plastic binder containing car registration and warranty; and one plastic stacked picnic set.

Any clues or information you may have regarding this disappearance would be deeply appreciated.

Please contact your local R.C.M.P.

Thank you,
Concerned Friends"

Nearly 20,000 flyers were taken to the post office on Wednesday, October 27, 1971, and the postmaster assured us the delivery would be completed by Friday, the 29th. All of the $600 needed for mailing came from generous donors all over Alberta. The flyers did produce many new leads, but, as it turned out, the break that Staff Sergeant Poss was looking for came in a rather unexpected fashion the following day from a location far from the areas we had covered with our flyers.

My phone rang on the night of October 31 and once again it was Detective Gowler's voice. He didn't say "trick or treat," either. Something new had developed, which he would tell me if I would be sure not to say anything to anyone. They wanted to keep all unnecessary traffic out of the area and so wanted no publicity at all.

His story was this: Two hunters chasing game birds had come upon MaryAnn's briefcase in the Fort Assiniboine area. The R.C.M.P. were there searching with dogs and he would also be going.

James Boyd and Max Leigrand had discovered the case in what police consider to be a "one-in-a-million chance" on October 30, 1971. Upon opening it, they had realized whose it was and had immediately contacted the Swan Hills R.C.M.P. detachment. An immediate search involving men, dogs, and aircraft had then been initiated.

The briefcase had been found behind three pines about fifty feet from the road, almost as though it had simply been thrown in from the roadway. The all-weather road led to the Pinto Creek Sawmill on

128

Goose Lake, about eighteen miles south and west of Fort Assiniboine.

During the search the dogs uncovered a cache of papers and things from the car about a mile from where the briefcase was, on the same side of the road and about the same distance into the bush. The cache had been well hidden.

Between October 30th and November 4th, as many as twenty-eight men and four dogs scoured a total of twelve miles along that road. The dogs went first. Then the men, spaced five yards apart for fifty yards on both sides of the road, did their best to make as fast and as thorough a search as possible. They were working against time because the skies were threatening snow every day.

It was during that weekend that I experienced another wonderful answer to prayer. Because I was not free to share the news with anyone, I did the only thing open to me. I talked to God about it and asked Him simply to impress, on whomever He could, the need to pray right then.

I learned much later of at least three people who during that very weekend had awakened in the middle of the night with a strong urge to pray for me and for the situation in general. One was in Washington, one was in Medicine Hat, and one was in Edmonton. None of them knew each other and none of them knew of the new developments, but all of them knew God, and in answer to my prayer, He had placed on them the burden to pray.

On November 5th, four inches of snow fell on the Judy Creek area and brought the search to a halt. The things that had been found I was able to identify as belonging to MaryAnn. The searchers, digging up several fresh mounds of dirt, had unearthed animal remains buried by hunters, but nothing more pertaining to the case.

After that I resigned myself to a long wait through

129

the winter. The police said that the high grass and dense brush made searching very difficult and four inches of snow made it virtually impossible to do a thorough job. As it turned out, they had come to within about a mile and a half of where MaryAnn's body had been dumped. Further routine checks by the police were made between November 10-13, November 27-30, and December 22-January 5. These were not prompted by any new evidence, but were concentrated in the areas where the briefcase and the papers had been discovered.

Meanwhile the R.C.M.P. and the Edmonton City Police Force checked many new leads and investigated many suspects. All the leads ended without success and all the suspects were cleared.

The next big breakthrough came in the spring. It was the discovery of MaryAnn's clothing. Then came the discovery of her remains. That brought the search for the victim to a successful, though tragic, conclusion.

But it did not end the search for the criminal. After the funeral, Corporal Hatch, who has since been promoted to Sergeant, and Detective Gowler were freed from all other duties to combine their forces on this one case alone. They worked through their files once more, going over every shred of information again, checking everything to make sure nothing had been overlooked. They were very thorough. I have on several occasions commented to friends that in my opinion Corporal Hatch has the tenacity of a bulldog. But in spite of all the efforts of Hatch and Gowler and all the others the criminal is still at large.

Because the case is still open, I have omitted several key aspects so as not to jeopardize future investigations that will be made. There is no way that one can measure the magnitude of such an investigation. Literally hundreds of man hours were put into the search. No one really knows the mileage travelled. The search covered all of Canada, the North West Territories, and some of the United States. The cost involved in the investigation was astronomical.

I asked Hatch and Gowler to give me a personal theory as to the motive and means of death. They were hesitant even to speculate, so I will do some speculating on my own. The possibility of sexual assault is always there and I know that MaryAnn would have fought like a tiger to avoid rape. That could have led to violence ending in death.

But looking back at how carefully Cooper set her up I get the impression that he was some "kook" with something to prove to himself. He carefully developed her confidence. He made sure he was never seen by anyone who might have been able to finger him later. He left no phone number or address through which he could be traced. I think he may have had a perverted desire to prove to himself that he could kill and get away with it. He needed a victim and MaryAnn happened to be the one he chose.

Several other things seem obvious to me. Cooper would have had to be familiar with the Real Estate business and know that agents willingly pick up their clients as a service. It just makes good business sense. He would have had to be familiar with the area in which he disposed of the body and belongings. He could have lived there; maybe he still does. He could have worked there, vacationed there, hunted or fished there, but he would have had to know the area. The possibility of his finding that area by chance after the initial crime is very remote indeed. Some of MaryAnn's belongings are still missing, like shoes, glasses, tan-tooled leather purse with all her identification, two pairs of sunglasses in brown leather cases, and a complete set of keys in a brown, handmade case. He had to be either foolish or very brazen to drive as far as he did with a body in the trunk and then drive the car right past the office on the way in. Yet a man like that could easily be your next door neighbor.

As to the means of death, again we cannot be entirely sure. Her body, of course, had decomposed long before it was discovered. The autopsy ruled out death by head injury. Had she been stabbed or shot in the body there would surely have been more blood in the trunk. That leaves only the possibility of strangulation. That is my theory of how she died.

And what about the future? Both men have indicated that their files will remain open. They are checked periodically as a matter of routine. Corporal Hatch, looking over the three heavy folders lying on his desk, once said to me with a grin, "They will probably give me these as a going-away present when I retire, if I can't solve the case before then." When I talked to him just recently, he mentioned that several new leads are being investigated at this moment. I am still confident that "the bulldog" will win. After all, just recently the media reported that in British Columbia a man was convicted for a murder he had committed twenty years ago.

One day the man who cast the shadow over our lives will see a shadow fall across his path and will look into the face of a policeman. Until then, he will be looking over his shoulder every minute of his life.

VII

DISPELLING THE SHADOWS

The longest winter of my life was finally giving way to spring. As each day lengthened, the sun seemed to shine with greater intensity. The ground, which had been covered by snow for five months, slowly began to emerge again as the spring runoff increased from tiny trickles to muddy streams.

We had already lived in the shadows for six months and there seemed to be no end in sight. However, with the coming of spring, there came to my inner being some new feelings.

When the first snow in the Fort Assiniboine area had fallen on November 5, 1971, I had resigned myself to a long wait. But as I watched the snow disappear, there arose within me a new feeling of hope that soon the search would be resumed and the end would be forthcoming. However, the snow melted much more rapidly within the city limits than it did in the dense bush.

I sensed along with my renewed hope a new feeling of inner restlessness that I could not explain and could hardly control. The urge to search was nearly overwhelming. Every bare patch of grass, every stream flowing with increasing force, every clump of trees and bushes seemed to beckon me, almost dared me, to come and search for some new evidence that might lay concealed beneath the cold blanket of snow.

But the restlessness went deeper than that. I had waited patiently for a long time, yet in the spring it seemed that I faced an additional test of patience. While I didn't want to be impatient with the Lord, the restlessness within me was almost more than I could endure. About two weeks before the end came I sat in our prayer meeting at the church and shared with the group my restless feeling. I asked them to pray that I would endure. I went home that night reassured that these friends would help to carry my load with specific prayer on my behalf.

When I look back now, I believe it was the Lord's way of partially preparing me for the next event in that long walk through the Valley of Shadows. Because of my restlessness, I began to be more specific in my prayers that the end would come soon. It was almost as though I had a premonition that something was about to happen. Yet, when it did, the end came with almost the same shocking swiftness as the beginning.

I had worked all winter on a construction project at Ninety-Second Street and 144th Avenue. It was now almost complete and by April 17th the snow was all gone. There was still some mud around, but it was dry enough to clean up the construction site. My father-in-law, Metro Sherstan, had been hired by the company to help with the cleanup, so we were working together that day. Needless to say, we talked about the one concern that was uppermost in our minds. He wanted to know if I had heard anything more from the police. I hadn't. While we worked and talked I could hardly contain my restless soul. That afternoon something happened that was to change my life completely. The shadows were about to lift.

There was still on the site a construction shack with

134

a phone in it. The phone was used only for outgoing calls because no one was ever there to answer any incoming calls. At about one-thirty or two o'clock, I suddenly had an impulse to try to call my boss. But just as I reached the shack, the phone began to ring.

"Good afternoon—Engineered Homes," I said.

"Corporal Hatch speaking. Is Mr. Jake Plett there, please?"

"Speaking."

"Oh, Mr. Plett, there has been a new development in the case. Someone has found some clothing that we think might have belonged to MaryAnn. Could you come down to the station to see if you can identify it? Oh, and a woman's watch was also found. It's a silver-colored watch, a Bulova, with an expansion bracelet. The bracelet is broken."

"That sounds like hers. What about the clothing?"

"There is part of a brown, orange, and beige top like you described to us. Parts of a beige or light tan pair of slacks and a blue cloth coat."

"When can I see them? How about if I come right after work? I work until four-thirty and I could come after that."

"Fine, Mr. Plett. Just give the commissionaire at the door my name and he will call me."

After he had hung up the receiver, I stood there in that shack in a daze. Could it be possible that finally the end was in sight? Was I finally going to be able to walk out of the shadows into the light again? I was glad for the new evidence, of course, because of the hope that it held for resolving the long-standing mystery of MaryAnn's whereabouts. But at the same time I was filled with a new sense of foreboding that the worst that we had feared was about to be verified.

I finally went back to work again, but my mind certainly did not seem to be with my body. I was aching to tell Mr. Sherstan what I had just heard, but thought better of it. I figured I had better wait until I could identify the clothing before raising his hopes that the end was in sight. Those last few hours of work seemed endless.

Before I left for home I called MaryAnn's brother at the service station and asked if he would go with me to the police station. He was glad to. At home, Mrs. LeGrand, my housekeeper, graciously consented to stay until I got back, which meant that she would have to keep supper for me. She always had it ready when I came home.

Just before going to the station I went upstairs to the dresser. In one of the drawers was a piece of material that had been left over from the multicolored top that MaryAnn had worn on her last day. She had sewn it herself.

There was no doubt at all about whose clothing had been found. The piece of material I had matched exactly with that which Corporal Hatch showed me. The materials found also included pieces of her coat and slacks, a button from her top, her watch, and a few other small items. I was sure the watch was hers, but to leave no trace of doubt they checked it out with the jewelry store in Two Hills, Alberta where it had been purchased as a high school graduation gift to MaryAnn from her parents. The jeweler's record confirmed that it was hers, purchased from him more than ten years earlier.

How had the new discovery come about? Corporal Hatch filled in the details. On Friday, April 14, 1972, two workmen from the Pinto Creek Sawmill had been doing some drainage work along the road. Just off to one side in a small patch of grass where the sun had penetrated the snow cover and melted the snow they had noticed some clothing. The men had been very much aware of the importance of such a discovery

136

because it had been along that road that all the searching had been done the preceding fall. They had reported the find to their boss, who had then immediately called the Swan Hills R.C.M.P.

"What happens now?" I asked.

"We plan to go in again on Wednesday with a tracking dog to see what we can find," said the Corporal.

That was Monday. I didn't know how I would be able to wait through the next two days. We told MaryAnn's parents that evening and tried as gently as possible to prepare them for what seemed to be inevitable. I don't know why I made an exception, but that was the one-and-only time I didn't tell the boys the news right away.

I went to bed that night with mixed emotions. I was impatient because I still had two days to wait. I was glad because I was reasonably sure the end was in sight. But I was sad because I had very little doubt about what the outcome would be.

The next morning I was up in plenty of time for my morning meditations in my study. I sat down at my desk, bowed my head and said, "Lord, I need something from You this morning. Something that will give me an indication of what I might expect." I picked up my **Good News for Modern Man**, the modern-language New Testament I used in my reading.

A few days before I had begun reading in Matthew's Gospel and that morning I came to chapter seven. When I got to verse seven my mind was arrested by what I read: "Ask, and you will receive; seek, and you will find; knock, and the door will be opened to you. For everyone who asks will receive, and he who seeks will find, and the door will be opened to him who knocks" (Matthew 7:7,8).

I trembled as I read those words over and over

again. They were directed to me in my special need that morning of April 18, 1972. I took a red pen and underlined the verses. Then slowly I doubled the lines under the words that offered me new hope: "...you will receive...you will find...the door will be opened to you."

Very quietly, with tears coursing down my cheeks, I said, "Lord, today I am asking You for one thing. When Corporal Hatch and Detective Gowler go into the search area with their police dog tomorrow, let them find the evidence that will bring an end to our agonizing uncertainty. Lord, I am now simply waiting to receive." I arose and went about my daily duties confident that the time had come.

The next morning, however, found me back in my study again. When I picked up my New Testament, I bowed my head and said, "Lord, just give me one more word of assurance today to strengthen my faith and renew my confidence." Then I turned my attention to the next chapter, Mattthew 8. And the Lord in His kindness doubled the assurance.

The first four verses told of Jesus' encounter with a leper who said, " 'Sir, if you want to, you can make me clean.' Jesus reached out and touched him. 'I do want to,' he answered. 'Be clean.' At once he was clean from his leprosy" (Matthew 8:2,3,). I put myself in the leper's place and simply told the Lord the same thing about my situation. If He wanted to, He could that day unfold the mystery that had haunted us for so long. I sensed that He was giving me the same answer—"You will know today."

As I continued to read, I read the account of a Roman officer whose servant was ill. He went to Jesus and simply told him his problem and expressed his confidence that Jesus could restore the servant's health. What impressed me most, and what I underlined in red, was the answer Jesus gave him: "Go home, and what you believe will be done for you. And the officer's servant was healed that very hour" (Matthew 8:13).

Jesus tested his faith. He didn't say, "Your servant is well." He said, "You will get what you have faith to receive." I closed my Bible and said simply, "Thank you, Lord. I know that today is the day when we will know the answer."

One other incident happened that morning, an incident which clinched my confidence. The boys and I always had our family Bible devotions at breakfast. We would read a portion from the Bible and pray together. When we had finished that morning I looked up and the older boy was crying. I said, "Nelson, what's the matter?" Through his tears he sobbed, "I want my mommy." I thought it rather strange that after seven months he should suddenly break up like that for no apparent reason—unless it was the Lord's kind way of preparing them for the next bit of news that was to come that evening.

And then I remembered. I hadn't told them about the discovery of the clothing. So there at the breakfast table I told them what had happened on Monday at the police station and that the police were going to search again that day. And so it was that in spite of my oversight the boys had at least one day to prepare themselves for what lay just ahead.

I went to work that day in complete confidence that the day of discovery had dawned. Later that morning I called Mom Sherstan and told her, "Today is the day."

"How do you know?" she asked.

I told her what I had read that morning and the day before. I told her about Nelson and his feelings. There was no doubt in my mind at all. Later that afternoon I was working with Mr. Sherstan and, of

139

course, we discussed again the one topic closest to both of us. He stood on one side of the truck and I on the other. I leaned over the side and said, "Dad, today is the day they will find her."

"How do you know?" he asked.

I repeated to him what I had read the last two mornings and said again, "I just know it will be today."

Mrs. LeGrand had supper ready as usual when I got home that afternoon. She left and we ate our supper with the usual light chatter about the day's happenings at school and at work. I cleared the table and sat down in my chair in the living room to read the paper. I was just settled when the phone rang.

"Hello." It was a familiar voice, very quiet, but on that occasion its effect was electrifying.

"Hello, Jake, Al Gowler here." He started with the usual light talk about various things, while I waited for him to tell me what I really wanted to know. Finally he said, "Well, I guess we found what we didn't want to find."

"Is that right?" I asked.

"Yes," he said. "We took the dog to the spot where the clothing was found and it didn't take him long to find the rest."

I said, "I knew you would find her." He was surprised, so I told him the same story I had told Mr. and Mrs. Sherstan earlier that day. Then he was no longer surprised, because he believes in the same God I do.

There still remained the important matter of positive identification. I asked if I could be there. "You can," he said, "but if you would rather not, it isn't that necessary. I won't be there, but if you wish I'll tell Corporal Hatch you are coming." I assured him that I wanted to go for my own sake.

For one thing, I wanted to be fully convinced in my

own mind that there had been no mistake. The other reason was that I felt I needed to go in order to be able to properly sever my own emotional ties from one who had been an integral part of my life for ten years.

I believe it was about 7:00 P.M. when we arrived at the R.C.M.P. station. Once again I had called on Bill, MaryAnn's brother, to go with me. He stood by me in that hour just as firmly as he had through all those trying months. The commissionaire let us in and called for Corporal Hatch. Once more we walked with him down the long corridor to the area where his office was. It was a large central square surrounded on all sides by private offices.

I was somewhat apprehensive, knowing that the task would not be pleasant. As I looked at Corporal Hatch his face registered the unpleasantness of his duty. He opened the door of a small, white fridge and lifted out a green, plastic bag. He set it on the desk and opened it. There before me lay the few remains of one of the most beautiful persons I have ever known.

While I was reasonably convinced, Corporal Hatch was still not satisfied. "Who was her dentist?" he asked.

"Dr. John Woytuck," I replied. "He lives in Sherwood Park. He should have all her records." While we waited for him, we talked a bit about the day's happenings, but mostly we just sat, without words, each alone with his own thoughts.

The three of us stood and watched intently as Dr. Woytuck took his chart and very slowly and deliberately checked every tooth against the chart, first from one side and then back again. No one said a word. Slowly he raised his head. He was visibly pale and shaken. "Gentlemen," he said, "there is absolutely no question but that this is Mrs. Plett."

141

We asked the Corporal not to release the news until the following morning. He agreed to wait until he had heard from us and then we left to face one of the most difficult assignments yet. We had to break the news to the immediate family and relatives.

Here, once again, we were aided by the fact that we were a praying family. Just two days before, while I was talking with Mom Sherstan, she had suggested that we call the extended family together for another evening of prayer. I had asked her to arrange it for Wednesday evening at my house. So when Bill and I arrived back home from the police station most of the local relatives were already there. They already knew where we had gone and why, so it was merely a matter of telling them the simple truth.

We walked into the living room and sat down. No one spoke for a few moments and the silence became heavy. Finally, someone managed the question everyone seemed afraid to ask—"Well, what's the news?"

"There is no doubt about it. They have found her body."

Once again heavy silence. A few broke into tears. It doesn't matter how well prepared one might think he is for such news, it still hits you hard when it first arrives. It's like a heavyweight's fist planted right in the midsection. When the initial shock was over, I asked, "Where are the boys?"

"They're still outside. Shall I go get them?"

"Yes, I'd like to tell them right away, by myself."

They were wide-eyed when they walked into the room. They knew something was wrong. I took them upstairs to their room, sat down beside them on the bed, and took a deep breath.

Then very simply and quietly I said, "Boys, I just came from the police station."

"Did they find Mommy?" The question came from

Nelson and his eyes lit up with hope.

"They found Mommy's body."

Tears rushed in and quenched the light in his eyes. He opened his mouth wide and gave vent to his anguish in the only way he knew. I did my best to comfort him. Lyndon just sat there without a word, suffering in silence, as he had done so often in the past seven months. Grandma Sherstan came up then to lend a hand. With the return of composure, we went back downstairs to begin notifying a list of relatives who lived farther away.

I made a call to a sister-in-law in Calgary. I said, "They found MaryAnn's body today. The funeral will be either Saturday or Monday. Would you make sure that everyone in my family knows? I'll leave that up to you. I hope you will be able to come."

We called MaryAnn's sisters: Nell Rodiuk in Medicine Hat, Alberta; Jeanne Foley in Tacoma, Washington; and Florence Daneliuk in Kodiak, Alaska. There were a few more local calls to be made and then the family spent some time in prayer. We offered our thanks to God that the agony of uncertainty was finally over and asked for strength to meet the strain and pressure of the new developments ahead.

The following morning I went to a few close neighbors and gave the news to them in person before the story broke in the media. When I came back, I called Corporal Hatch and said, "You can release the news. We have notified all relatives."

At ten o'clock that Thursday morning, April 20, 1972, the report came: "The body of Edmonton realtor, Mrs. MaryAnn Plett, was found yesterday in dense bush near Fort Assiniboine." I winced a little as the announcer went into a bit more detail.

143

That was the top news story every hour for almost a whole day. It was the first real break in three mysterious disappearances in the fall of 1971.

Before I go on to describe the days which followed, I would like to go back in time a few days to illustrate again what I have tried to show before—that God was firmly in control all the time. I have tried to show how prayer, simple but sincere, brought unusual results. I have stated that I believed that when God's time came, He would unravel the mystery. The fact is that the discovery of MaryAnn's body came as a direct result of prayer, not only my prayers, but also the prayers of others.

Mom and Dad Sherstan had gone to the Prairie Bible Institute in Three Hills, Alberta on the weekend of April 14-16 to participate in the school's annual Spring Conference. Hundreds of people come to Three Hills every year from all over North America to hear prominent Bible teachers and missionary leaders. On the Friday of the week-long conference, opportunity was given for members of the audience to share personal burdens or victories, whatever the case might be.

Mom Sherstan shared the heavy burden she and the family bore in regard to her daughter. When she had finished talking, the president of the school, Mr. L.E. Maxwell, who was in charge of the meeting, called on the audience to band together right then in earnest prayer for God to intervene. Immediately some four thousand people present in the Prairie Tabernacle that day engaged in united intercession. It is significant that that very day, April 14, 1972, several hundred miles away, two workmen found the clothing that led to the discovery of

144

MaryAnn's body. "The prayer of the righteous man has a powerful effect" (James 5:16). In this case hundreds of people were praying the world over and the powerful effect is unmistakably clear.

The days following the discovery were busy days indeed. All of the funeral arrangements had to be made immediately. We chose "Park Memorial" as our funeral directors since they had served the family very capably on previous occasions. We went to Evergreen Memorial Gardens to arrange for a plot. There was a plot available right next to the grave of MaryAnn's grandmother. Since MaryAnn had been very fond of her grandmother, I'm sure that if she had been able, she herself would have chosen that spot as her own, nestled as it was between her grandmother and her Uncle Nick.

Since our own congregation was meeting in a small, rented building at the time, we decided to hold the funeral service in Beulah Alliance Church, where MaryAnn's parents worship. The building seats about 900 to 1,000 when filled to capacity. Among the many details, we had to arrange for a speaker, soloist, organist, etc. I went through all of those concerns in a very mechanical manner, still trying to sort out my own feelings.

The funeral was held at ten o'clock on April 24, 1972, a dull, grey Monday morning. Some of the family arrived at my house about nine o'clock and mostly waited in silence for the funeral car to arrive. All of us sensed a feeling of great relief that at least the uncertainty was passed. The one expression that I heard more than any other expressed our feelings well—"At least we know now what happened."

Yet our feelings of relief in no way eased the sorrow and deep grief we all shared. There really are no words adequate to describe it. Before we left the church I spoke briefly to the boys. I wanted them to have at least some knowledge of what would happen next. Among other things, I said, "If you feel like crying, just go right ahead. Don't try to hold it back. Just make sure you have enough Kleenex in your pocket and try not to cry too loudly."

The funeral itself went smoothly, according to plan. The building was comfortably full. People had come from many walks of life. Of course, the Real Estate business was well represented. MaryAnn had made many friends among her business associates. Some of her many satisfied clients were there. Friends of the family on both sides and acquaintances too numerous to name had come, many of them from long distances.

We had planned the service carefully. We wanted an atmosphere of triumph, rather than despair, to permeate the service. We knew well the words of St. Paul: "Brothers, we want you to know the truth about those who have died, so that you will not be sad, as are those who have no hope. We believe that Jesus died and rose again; so we believe that God will bring with Jesus those who have died believing in Him" (I Thessalonians 4:13,14).

Certainly we grieved, but we grieved more for our own loss than for MaryAnn. The triumph was that MaryAnn had reached her heavenly home. We would see her again. And when we looked at her **gain**, instead of our **loss**, we were filled with a deep sense of peace, joy, and gratitude. When the congregation rose to sing the first hymn, "Safe in the Arms of Jesus," my heart nearly burst with joy.

Perhaps for the sake of custom, I resisted the urge to stand with the congregation and sing as loudly as I could, but I was too choked-up with emotion anyway. When the soloist, Rev. George Ross, sang his first song, I knew so well the meaning of its words:

My heart can sing when I pause to remember,
A heartache here is but a stepping stone.
Along the trail that's winding always upward,
This troubled world is not my final home.

Chorus:
But until then my heart shall go on singing,
Until then with joy I'll carry on.
Until the day my eyes behold the city,
Until the day God calls me home.

His second song, "He Giveth More Grace," was again so true of my experience and I had sung it myself so often. As he sang with deep feeling the words which tell of the limitless supply of God's grace available to all of His own, I sensed again, even at that moment, God's strength and grace being infused into my being. I took a special draught right then—because I had asked to be allowed to say a few words to the mourners on behalf of myself and the family. Not wanting to sound presumptuous, I had discussed what I wanted to say with various people beforehand. All had encouraged me to go ahead.

It is no easy thing to speak at your own wife's funeral. I had no desire to make a fool of myself, yet there I stood facing all those people and the mourning families. I took a deep breath and began to read what I wanted to say:

"'**Offer to God the sacrifice of thanksgiving, and pay your vows to the Most High; and call upon me in the day of trouble; and I will deliver you and you shall honor and glorify me.**'

"These words of the psalmist have prompted the family and me to publicly express our deep gratitude to God for the following things:

"(1) My personal gratitude to God for ten

147

wonderfully happy years of marriage." (When I came to the next sentence I nearly broke down. I stopped to regain my composure. One of my sisters told me afterwards that she had whispered, "Come on, Jake, you can do it." I didn't hear that whisper, but I swallowed hard, took another huge gulp of air, and proceeded.) "MaryAnn was a model companion, wife, and mother. In all our years together we never had any serious conflicts and we parted on the morning of September 15, 1971, with our lives in perfect harmony.

"(2) As a family, we are deeply grateful to God for relief from seven long months of agonizing uncertainty. The sorrow of parting is far less painful to us than the past experience of uncertainty.

"(3) We give glory to God that our confidence has not been shaken, because He has vindicated His name. All of the unsolicited predictions of the occultists have been proven false. How glad we are today that we did not weaken when during the deep trials they sought to involve us with the sinister powers of darkness. God's name today stands supreme above every other name in heaven or earth.

"(4) We give God thanks that we did not become bitter, and that He has enabled us to pray for the one who has burdened his own conscience by being responsible for the snuffing out of the life of one deeply loved and sorely needed by the family. We want him to know that God loves him and that when he calls upon God's forgiveness He will deliver him from guilt and give him the hope of eternal life.

"(5) We are grateful to God today for the glorious living hope of eternal life through the resurrection of the dead. Jesus said, 'I am the resurrection and the life. Whoever believes in me will live, even though he dies; and whoever lives and believes in me will never die.' We know that at this very moment while we meet to lay to rest the house of clay in which she lived for twenty-nine years, MaryAnn is rejoicing in the glorious presence of her Lord and Saviour, Jesus Christ, Who she knew personally and loved deeply. She now sees Him face to face. We also know that one day soon, 'There will be the shout of command, the archangel's voice, the sound of God's trumpet, and the Lord Himself will come from heaven. Those who died believing in Christ will be raised to life first. Then we who are living at the time will all be gathered up along with them in the clouds to meet the Lord in the air. And so we will always be together with the Lord. Therefore we cheer each other up with these words.'

"(6) Finally, we wish to express our gratitude to God for His sustaining grace which He has made so abundantly available to us during all these difficult months. We remember what the prophet Samuel said, 'Hitherto the Lord hath helped us.' It implies that His grace will continue to be available to us in superabundant measure in the days ahead. We offer God our thanks at this moment for His divine **wisdom**, to face difficult decisions; for His inexhaustible **grace**, through which He literally infused us with strength; for His wonderful **peace**, which is beyond human understanding; for His unfathomable **love**, so lavishly bestowed upon us; and for His **everlasting arms**, which have and always will enfold and uphold us.''

There was only the sound of a few quiet sniffles in the audience as Reverend Ed Enarson, a personal friend of mine, stood to give the address. He emphasized four main thoughts:
1. ''The Christian Life is built on the certainty of the

Scriptures'' (II Peter 1:19-21).

How well I knew the certainty and trustworthiness of the Word of God.

2. "The Christian Life is built on the certainty of the Personal Salvation" (II Timothy 1:12).

MaryAnn had committed her life to the Lord at four years of age and had lived in the assurance of eternal life from that time on.

3. "The Christian Life is built on the certainty of God-Controlled Circumstances."

Here, from his message, is his own explanation:

" 'We know that all things work together for good to those who love God, to those who are called according to His purpose' (Romans 8:28). The purpose of God is stated in the following verse. It is conformity to His Son. God, the Great Potter, takes us, the clay, and through the circumstances of life fashions us after the likeness of His own blessed Son.

"When tragedy struck Mr. Plett's home, I remember his sharing with me something I shall never forget. He said, 'I asked why, and for a time things seemed very dark, until I learned that a Christian must never ask WHY, but rather, WHAT. When I began asking God what He had in mind—that is to say, what was His purpose in allowing the event—my heart began to rest.'

"We have been able to witness some of these purposes in the many ways in which the cause of Christ has been forwarded by this seeming tragedy. We know as Christians that all things work together for our good and for God's glory because God Himself said so. In this confidence we can rest even though we may not understand.

4. "The Christian Life is built on the certainty of an eternal city" (II Corinthians 5:1).

Oh, the joy of knowing that MaryAnn had reached that eternal city. Though we wept that day for

150

ourselves, nothing could dim the joy of that certainty.

After the graveside ceremony, and after the lunch at the church provided by the Women's Missionary Society of the Evangelical Free Church, which both of us had attended regularly, we went home. Most of my relatives came over for awhile. The living room was filled with people and flowers. But after a few hours, one by one they all said, "Well, I think we had better go now. We still have a long way to go before we get home." They all lived several hundred miles away.

I don't blame them for going, but I was about to face another crisis. Before long, everyone was gone except my brother Corne and his wife, Ramona. I was tired and tense. Ramona is a certified nursing aid and so she suggested a good back rub. I lay down on the chesterfield and while we talked she worked all the knots out of my aching muscles. I don't think I have ever appreciated a good back rub more.

But I was stricken with a new and different sense of loneliness. All the ties that had united us for ten years were being severed at one time. I needed to get out of the house in a hurry. I went upstairs and changed my clothes. I took off my wedding band and laid it in the jewelry box among MaryAnn's things. As I was coming back downstairs, once again MaryAnn's brother Bill came to the rescue. I answered the phone and he suggested we all come over to their house for the evening. It helped to tide me over that first realization that I was now entirely on my own with two young boys to look after.

The days that followed were busy ones. While MaryAnn's family was still with us we decided to go through the whole house and remove all her personal belongings. Until then, everything was just as she had left it. First of all the boys each chose an

151

article to serve as a memento. I chose a few pictures and the things I wanted to keep for the boys and stored them in a trunk. Then each member of the family was free to choose what he wanted and the balance was packed away and delivered to Hope Mission to be used as the people in charge saw fit. There were no arguments and it was done as a final act of love for one of their own.

At long last we had emerged from the gloomy shadows of trial and uncertainty into higher prospects for the future. We would never forget her. But each of us would begin to restructure our lives again, to rebuild what had been shattered. The long shadows would lift gradually, over a period of time.

As I look back now, the dark shadows have been dispelled. But there are still a few lingering shadows that remain; not the dark, ominous kind, but shadows nonetheless. They still hover over our lives and occasionally succeed in dimming the light of our new-found happiness. They come mostly in the form of thoughts of what might have been if MaryAnn had lived. So many things have happened that would have keenly interested her.

She would have loved to have seen both boys dressed in full hockey uniforms for the first time and to have watched them learn to play the game. It was hilarious, but she was not there to enjoy it. She would be proud today to see the progress they have made. She would have been as proud as I was to see Lyndon come home from kindergarten with his graduation picture taken with him all dressed up in cap and gown. She would have been thrilled to read a letter from the girl who had been her best friend all through high school. She and her husband had tried for years to have a child, without success. Finally they had adopted a boy. She had written that she was expecting a child—but MaryAnn would never share that joy with her.

She had frequently talked about selling the duplex and buying another home. When my family moved in June, 1973 into our home in the Londonderry district the dimming shadows returned once again. I thought of all the happy memories that surrounded the duplex. As I walked through the empty house one final time to see that we hadn't left anything behind, I realized that I was leaving behind a house full of memories. I thought of how happy she would have been in the new house. But these are shadows I have learned to live with.

There is still another lingering shadow, though, that hovers around us. The man MaryAnn knew as "James Cooper" has not been apprehended up to the time of this writing. The police files are still open. And the haunting thought which comes back again and again is that somewhere, possibly even within the city of Edmonton, someone is sitting on information that would get a dangerous criminal off the streets.

Someone must have known him. On September 15, 1971, he had to be away from home from about 10:30 A.M. to after 11:00 P.M. Surely someone must have seen him come or go. I appeal to the conscience of anyone who might be withholding such information. Please come forward and make it known. One successful crime could be an invitation for another attempt. The next time it might be someone very close to you who has to suffer. Please help us to remove these lingering shadows by helping the police apprehend the man responsible for bringing them in the first place.

VIII

BEYOND THE SHADOWS

The shadows which had covered our lives for all those months were lifting at long last. To my surprise, I soon discovered that I would have to learn to cope with my sense of relief that it was finally over. I felt like a jack-in-the-box which had been held down under intense pressure for many months and then had been suddenly released. Like the sprung jack-in-the-box I was waving back and forth hardly knowing where to begin to reorganize. I wanted to reorganize our family life. I wanted to hear the sound of laughter in the home once again. We desperately needed a new sense of direction and meaning for our lives.

Naturally, at my age I would consider marrying again. I remembered an evening when MaryAnn was still alive, sitting around the kitchen table with Allan and Phyllis Reynar, discussing what each of us would do if death should ever take our partner. Both MaryAnn and Phyllis had felt that they would find it difficult to marry again. Al and I had both stated that we would probably remarry, and that we would probably do so within a year or so because of the domestic problems involved in being a widower with a family to support. Needless to say, we were not the most popular husbands that night and, of course, none of us had thought that we would ever face the possibility.

Yet there I was—less than two years later—a widower of seven months confronted by the very question we had discussed.

I began to consider the practical problems involved both in remaining single and in remarrying. First, I was desperately lonely, needing companionship. But could I expect to find another woman with whom I could live as happily as I had with MaryAnn? Aside from that, where would I find a woman who would be willing to accept the responsibilities involved in marrying a man who was in his middle thirties and who had two lively boys who would need a lot of attention? I didn't think it advisable to consider a woman who had children of her own. Then the relationship would be further complicated by "her" kids and "my" kids and possibly, in time, by "our" kids. But surely no single girl would be foolish enough to marry into such a situation. Yet I knew I was a father of two boys who would need more love and attention than my housekeeper, good as she was, could provide for them.

That presented another problem. When the Family Service Association had first sent Mrs. LeGrand to us as a daytime housekeeper, it was with the understanding that it was only a temporary service. That "temporary" service had by then extended to seven months and I really couldn't expect it to last much longer. I would have to make other arrangements. But what could I do? The boys had already remarked to others, "All Daddy knows how to cook is pancakes, eggs, and omelets!"

I had improved my cooking abilities a little, but certainly a cook I was not. Aside from cooking, someone had to be at home to see the boys off to school, since I left the house before eight. And certainly I couldn't leave them to shift for themselves when they came home in the afternoon.

But to hire someone to replace Mrs. LeGrand and to pay her the full going rate would take at least half my salary. (Mrs. LeGrand was being subsidized by the Family Service Association.) Yet the possibility of being married before the "temporary" housekeeper had to leave was at that point very remote indeed.

In addition, there was another matter which required some thought. Public opinion can sometimes be a persuasive force in formulating one's own opinions on certain issues. When it comes to such matters as remarriage after being widowed, public opinion generally holds that one should wait a "respectable" length of time before even considering such a step.

However, in my case, after the funeral various members of the family began to encourage me to think positively about remarriage because of the many practical problems that a widower with a family encounters. Even before MaryAnn's body was found, I had discussed the problem frankly with several members of my family and my in-laws, and there was general agreement that if MaryAnn were no longer living I would have to consider remarriage for the sake of my boys.

I remembered what Lyndon had said to me a few days after his mother had disappeared. "If we don't find Mommy, are we going to get another one?" I had answered, "Well, we won't worry about that now. We'll just hope we find her again." But now the time had come to think seriously about it.

As with all the other decisions we had to make during those days in the shadows, that one too received specific attention in prayer. Mom Sherstan confided in me on several occasions, "I'm just praying that if MaryAnn is gone, the Lord will direct you in finding a fine Christian girl whom He has prepared to take her place."

I had often prayed privately that if indeed I were a widower, the Lord would prepare me for the decisions that I would need to make in my quest for a new partner. I would need wisdom far beyond my own to make decisions that would affect our lives for many years to come.

I discovered later that on the very weekend in which I met for the first time my present wife, Marion, several families I knew well were praying specifically that God would provide a fine Christian woman to enter my life. As I look back now over the sequence of events which occurred I see again just how clearly the Lord guided.

I thought back to 1957 when I was confronted with the decision of whether or not I should enter Bible College. One evening a layman from the church I was attending took me aside after the service and said, "You know, the Lord guides us much like we steer a car. You can't steer a car unless it's in motion. In the same way, the Lord will guide you once you begin to move in a given direction. He may stop you, or move you to one side or the other, but only as you begin to move and remain sensitive to His leading."

Those few words became part of my way of living. Often, when I have faced a major decision, I have proceeded in the following way: I have followed what seemed to be the most normal course of action, but I have done so with the prayer that if my decision were not God's will, He would stop me in my tracks. I have told God that unless He convinced me otherwise, I would continue to pursue the path of my original decision.

Once again I made with God the same arrangement. I would begin to become acquainted with young ladies I considered eligible, and I would continue to develop a friendship into a courtship, unless, through circumstances of one kind or another, He very clearly put a stop to my procedure.

As it happened, a decision made immediately following the funeral was what led me to my present wife. We had decided that in lieu of flowers, donations could be given to the Gideons International in Canada for their program of placing memorial Bibles in motels, hotels, and schools. There was an overwhelming response and after the funeral I had a long list of people who together had contributed well over 300 Bibles in memory of MaryAnn.

The need to send thank-you notes to all those friends seemed like an insurmountable task. I knew at least five eligible young ladies and one of them happened to be a secretary in one of the government offices downtown. I had met her only once or twice very casually and knew only her first name. Consequently, I had to call her minister to get her full name and phone number.

To my surprise, when I called Marion Jeanne Craggs, she agreed to come the following evening, Monday, May 1st, to help me with the volume of correspondence. She typed the whole list of names in alphabetical order, along with the numbers of Bibles donated, so that all I had to do was go down the list and send out thank-you cards. She told me later how nervous she had been coming over that night, wondering how a young lady carries on a conversation with an older man.

I was coaching a little league baseball team that summer. We had had a game that night and didn't get home as soon as I had expected. Marion was waiting in her little blue Toyota when we returned. She needn't have worried about the conversation, because I think I did all the talking that evening. I made some tea and we talked for a while after the typing was done. I think we both knew that night that the relationship could easily develop into a permanent one, even though we were hesitant to say anything.

We both recognized that the decision would not be an easy one because there were three "men" involved. Her mother was in Vancouver when Marion wrote to her, but she came home in a hurry to find out what this strange old man wanted with her young daughter.

I was interested in what the boys would say the next morning. Their reactions were typical.

Nelson asked, "Is that lady going to be our new mommy?"

"Would you like her to be?"

"Yeah!" came his immediate response.

But Lyndon, who makes friends much more slowly than his brother, was not so sure.

I told the boys I wasn't sure who our new mommy would be, but that we would work it out together. They thought that would be fun!

On Thursday of that week Marion looked after the boys and put them to bed while I was out to a meeting. It gave us another opportunity to observe the boys' reactions. Typically, Nelson was open and friendly; Lyndon was quiet and withdrawn. As time went on, Marion and I both agreed that if our relationship was going to work at all it would have to be right for the two of us and for both the boys. We agreed to take the boys on some of our dates and to go on some of our dates alone.

One morning over breakfast, the boys and I were again talking about the possibilities of a new mother. Nelson was all for asking Marion. Lyndon still wasn't sure. I said, "If you want her, you are going to have to tell her so, because I won't ask her to become your mother unless I know that you really want her."

Several days later Marion was upstairs tucking them into bed. She said good night to Nelson, who hugged her without hesitation. He had done so before. Then came Lyndon's turn. As Marion bent over him, he lay there and looked up for awhile and then like a flash both arms just shot up and he nearly choked her. The ice was broken. From then on we both felt free to consider our relationship seriously.

So it was that on June 3, 1972 we became engaged and set the wedding date for August 12. Admittedly, everything was happening very quickly, but we packed a lot of getting acquainted into a short time. If we didn't see each other every day, we talked on the phone for up to an hour at night.

About a month before the wedding, the supervisor from the Family Service Association called again. She felt it was time to terminate the "temporary" service that they were providing. Could I come and see her? She had some other alternatives to suggest.

"I'm getting married on August 12," I said. "I was hoping she could stay on till then."

I don't think it registered on her right away. "Mrs. LeGrand is going on holidays in August," she continued, "and we should make other arrangements."

I repeated what I had said, "I'm getting married on August 12." As it turned out, that was the very weekend that Mrs. LeGrand's holidays were to begin, so even that worked out better than any of us could have hoped.

The wedding was attended mainly by our relatives and some friends from our respective churches. The ceremony was in the Missionary Church on 142nd Street and 104th Avenue, which Marion had attended. The reception was held in the gym of the Evangelical Free Church on 84th Avenue and 104th Street, where I was a member.

Many aspects of that wedding were new and different because of the particular situation. Nelson and Lyndon were as proud as they could be to be ring bearers at their "parents' " wedding. I think the prize picture has to be the one of Marion and the boys, with both boys looking up at her with beaming faces. It just did my heart good to see it.

At the reception we added something rather unusual. We had invited the Sherstan families and they had come. We wanted to keep our relationship with them as normal and natural as possible. They still considered the boys and me as part of the family and were willing to welcome Marion too.

So first of all, I presented Nelson and Lyndon to Mom Craggs as her grandchildren, making her an instant grandmother. (After all, this is the age of instant everything!)

Then with deep feeling I presented Marion to Mr. and Mrs. Sherstan, asking them to accept her as their daughter. She would never replace their daughter, MaryAnn, but she would have a place all her own in their hearts and as a member of the family. I am happy to report that this relationship has worked out exceedingly well. I must say that I respect both Marion and all the Sherstans for the way in which they have turned a potentially difficult situation into a happy relationship.

We took one week for our honeymoon in Penticton,

British Columbia, arriving back in Edmonton in time for the beginning of the new school term. The boys were staying with their Uncle Bill and Auntie Olga Sherstan. When we pulled up to their house both boys were waiting for us on the sidewalk. They opened the door and mobbed Marion before she could get out of the car. I don't think we will ever forget the first words Lyndon said. He threw his arms around her and said, "Now you are finally our mom."

There were those who felt that I had been in an awful hurry to remarry. I admit that it was sudden, but it was almost a year after I had lost MaryAnn. However, all those who knew the problems involved were in agreement that I was doing the right thing. To my knowledge only those who had never experienced such a situation and were not close enough to know all that was involved felt otherwise. At any rate, I was not too concerned about what people said. I had a new life to live.

Then came the period of settling in. I must say that as a young bride, Marion had many more things to cope with than most others. But to make matters even worse, we walked into a house that had its basement in shambles. On the night of our rehearsal, we had had a tremendous downpour of rain. When I had come home at midnight with my brother and his family and a niece and nephew, we had discovered to our dismay that the basement was flooded. We had spent most of the night mopping up water and cleaning up the mess. The rumpus room was carpeted wall to wall. We had had to throw out all the underlay. In the basement bedroom, a rug five-feet-by-seven-feet had been ruined, so we had thrown that out too.

Since the wedding was the next day, I had not been

able to clean up properly. When we returned from our honeymoon, the first thing we had to do was clean up the mess in the basement. The whole house smelled musty. We started in one corner and washed everything with Lysol. When we were done we called the city and workmen came and disinfected the whole basement. May I advise any new groom that that is not the ideal way to establish a new household?

We had decided earlier that when Marion moved in after the wedding she would be free to rearrange the household to suit her own taste. Naturally, we used "our" things instead of what had been there before. It took me quite awhile to get used to the new way the cupboards were arranged. Sometimes I had to hunt for quite awhile to find what I was looking for!

Although things didn't always go smoothly, I do think as I look back that we adjusted to each other better than either of us could have hoped. After all, there was more than a decade of years between us. I had previously been married for ten years, and had been accustomed to a fixed routine. Marion had to cope not only with one man, as most brides do, but with three of them, all of whom were used to doing things in a certain way.

There were more major adjustments to be made and there was humour, too. For example, for ten years, the bathroom tissue had rolled from the top down. Suddenly it began to roll from the bottom up. Since we had two baths, we compromised. Upstairs, the tissue rolled one way, downstairs the opposite way. Luckily, when it came to toothpaste we were both "end rollers." I don't know if I could have coped with a "tube squeezer."

Of course, one of the more major adjustments

Marion had to make was to fill her new role as instant mother. The boys had voluntarily started to call her "Mom" from the time we were engaged. But now she was in the home in the full role as their mother. It wasn't long before it became necessary to exercise discipline.

At first she would pass the responsibility on to me. But the time came when she had to begin rising personally to the challenges the boys threw out to her. I honestly think they tested her to see if she would really be able to fulfill the complete role as mother, including discipline. She tried several forms of correction until we both agreed that it was time for her to use the strap.

I still firmly believe that a pat on the back is very beneficial if it is done at the right time, in the right attitude, often enough, young enough, hard enough, and low enough. The first time Marion spanked them was somewhat symbolical because she didn't really lean into it. But soon the boys realized that she loved them enough to keep them in line. She cared about what happened to them.

On one occasion after she had spanked Nelson hard, he had immediately thrown his arms around her neck and sobbed through his tears, "I love you, Mommy." She had earned the right to be their mother and they have never called her by any other name. Right from the beginning, and even now when she and I have our playful arguments, the boys almost without fail side with their "mother."

While I was convalescing from surgery, the boys would leave for school in the morning and say, "Bye, Mom." I would say, "Bye, boys" and then they would suddenly remember I was home. "Bye, Dad." When they came home for lunch or after school, they would walk in the door, even after five weeks, and say, "Hi, Mom." Sometimes Marion wasn't home, or if she was, I would answer first— "Hello!" The immediate question which invariably came then was, "Where's Mom?" I think it was just another interesting commentary on the fact that Marion has filled her role in our home better than anyone could have expected.

A new cause for great excitement in our household came with the announcement that there would be a new member of the family in February, 1974. We hoped for a girl, of course. We have answered so many questions about babies that it would take another whole chapter to cover them all! Lyndon even asked one day if he could take the baby to "show and tell" at school. To add to the anticipation, Marion's identical twin sister, Marilyn, was expecting her baby two weeks before our due date.

Nine months can be a long time to wait, especially when what you are waiting for is something you want very much. Both boys were bursting with impatience. (Marilyn's baby girl, Cynthia Ruth, finally arrived on February 9, 1974, twelve days past her scheduled arrival. She weighed in at 7 pounds, 2 ounces and made us just that much more excited about our baby, still unborn.)

The day finally came, eight days later than we had first expected. Marion woke me at five-thirty and indicated that she thought the time had arrived. We discussed the situation for a few minutes and then decided it was time to act. I slipped quietly into the boys' room. "Boys," I said, "get up and get dressed right away. I'll take you to Collins' before I take Mommy to the hospital."

Both of them were awake in an instant. Lyndon sat

bolt upright in his bed and asked, "Is Mommy going to have her baby today?"

"I think so," I replied.

He then gave vent to all the pent-up emotions he had tried so hard to contain. He jumped out of bed, threw both arms up over his head, and yelled, "Yahoo!"

The delivery went very smoothly. I was with Marion, first in the labour room and later in the case room, throughout the delivery. Aside from the obvious pain for a mother giving birth, I think that to watch one's own child being born has to be one of the most beautiful experiences of life. I watched while Nelson was born. With Lyndon, everything happened so suddenly I hadn't made it in time. Now I watched in wonder as Carlene Marie arrived at 10:17 A.M., February 20, 1974. She weighed 7 pounds, 13 ounces. She is a beautiful girl with lots of hair and has already brought us much happiness.

The boys are eager to hold her whenever they can and we often hear things like, "He got to hold her twice already today and I haven't held her yet." Or, "He held her longer than I did." They have their sister, and they want to make the best of every moment. She is indeed a bright ray of sunshine in our lives and in our home.

The whole experience of remarriage and the readjustments we had to make have taught me some new lessons. At first I found it very easy to compare the skills and attributes of the two first ladies of my life. That practice is dynamite and I soon learned that I had to accept each as her own person, in her own right. MaryAnn had been a wonderful woman, with her own personality and abilities, but that was all in the past. Marion has her own personality and skills and she is in the present. There are similarities and there are differences, but to compare one woman with the other is unfair. I appreciate Marion's patience with me, especially at the beginning as I learned to cope with the temptation to make comparisons. Gradually the expression "We used to" disappeared from my conversation.

Another thing we both learned is that we could not avoid the past, so we learned to talk freely about all aspects of our past life without feeling threatened by it. It is simply unavoidable. It was a fact of our lives and to try to hide it would only bring other difficulties. It took some time, but we made the adjustment well.

Marion has also shared my interest in writing this book. While she found it difficult at times, she has done all the typing for me. She does make an excellent secretary besides being a wonderful wife, companion, and mother.

There are occasions even now, though, when we run into unpleasant incidents as a result of the past. When, for example, we began to consider buying a house this spring, Marion had occasion to call several Real Estate agents regarding properties they had listed for sale. One of them, when my wife identified herself as Marion Plett, just blurted out, "Did you come back from the dead?" I don't think we even went to look at his property.

But on the whole, I believe our adjustments have been made very well, considering all the pitfalls that can befall a marriage like ours. We are very happy as a family, which is really all that matters. Looking now from the broad plateau of happiness back over our journey through the deep darkness, I can still hear the Lord say, "This plan of mine is not what you would work out, neither are my thoughts the same as yours. For just as the heavens are higher than the earth, so are my ways higher than yours and my thoughts than yours" (Isaiah 55:8,9 LB).

I must admit that my journey through the dark shadows is not the way I would have chosen. But if God needed my suffering to help fulfill His purposes, I can only echo the words of the sweet psalmist of Israel, "As for God, His way is perfect" (Psalm 18:30, Amplified). Some day we will understand perfectly the purposes that God fulfilled by leading us through the Valley of Shadows.

Other HORIZON HOUSE books you will immensely enjoy

MY GOD CAN DO ANYTHING by Clarence Shrier is an amazing account of God's healing intervention in one man's life. Some stories are just incredible—this one is true. 96 pages, paper, $1.50.

TALL TALES THAT ARE TRUE by British Columbia Storyteller Arthur H. Townsend. A fascinating collection of crisply written short stories with spiritual applications. **A Million-Dollar Bonfire, The Pig Was Insured,** and many others. An excellent gift. 96 pages, paper, $1.50.

CARIBOO COUNTRY SAINTS AND SHENANIGANS by British Columbia Storyteller Arthur H. Townsend. The true story of the author's experiences and acquaintances as a pioneer preacher in a unique part of Canada. A rustic, romantic, authentic account of pioneer faith and fun. 160 pages, paper, $1.95.

BEYOND THE TANGLED MOUNTAIN by Douglas C. Percy is an authentic African novel by an award-winning Canadian *author. From his pen spins a fascinating web of missionary heroism, romance, tension and tragedy. Douglas Percy is one of the "best" on Africa. First time in paperback. 160 pages, paper, $1.95.*

PREACHERS, PRIESTS, AND CRITTERS edited by Eric Mills. An absorbing collection of unusual accounts. The rough-and-tumble speech of camp meetings is presented in a fascinating manner. Chapter titles include "The Flask that Wouldn't Break," "The Widow-Maker Missed Me," "Rotten Egged," and more. 96 pages, paper, $1.50.

CHOCOLATE CAKE AND ONIONS... WITH LOVE by Marilynne E. Foster is a collection of recipes that she has discovered in her own use to be tasty and easy to prepare. The love comes in selected excerpts from many writings about the theme of love. 96 pages, spiral spine, paper, $1.75.

Ask for these books from your bookseller. Or order them directly from HORIZON HOUSE PUBLISHERS, Box 600, Beaverlodge, Alberta, Canada. Please include 15 cents for postage and handling for each book ordered.